Nine American Jewish Thinkers

Books by Milton R. Konvitz

Author

On the Nature of Value
The Alien and the Asiatic in American Law
The Constitution and Civil Rights
Civil Rights in Immigration
Fundamental Liberties of a Free People: Religion, Speech, Press, Assembly
A Century of Civil Rights
Expanding Liberties
Religious Liberty and Conscience
Judaism and the American Idea
Torah and Constitution: Essays in American Jewish Thought
Nine American Jewish Thinkers

Editor

Bill of Rights Reader: Leading Constitutional Cases
*First Amendment Freedoms: Selected Cases
on Freedom of Religion, Speech, Press, Assembly*
Judaism and Human Rights
The Recognition of Ralph Waldo Emerson
Emerson: A Collection of Critical Essays (with Stephen E. Whicher)
The American Pragmatists (with Gail Kennedy)
Freedom and Experience (with Sidney Hook)
Essays in Political Theory (with Arthur H. Murphy)
Aspects of Liberty (with Clinton Rossiter)
Law and Social Action: Selected Essays of Alexander H. Pekelis
Education for Freedom and Responsibility by Edmund Ezra Day
*Liberian Code of Laws; Liberian Code of Laws Revised;
Liberian Law Reports*

Nine American Jewish Thinkers

Milton R. Konvitz

Transaction Publishers • Rutgers University
New Brunswick (U.S.A.) and London (U.K.)

Library of Congress Catalog Number: 00-037388
ISBN: 0-7658-0028-4
Printed in the United States of America

Library of Congress Cataloging-in-Publication Data

Konvitz, Milton Ridvas, 1908-
    Nine American Jewish thinkers / Milton R. Konvitz.
        p. cm.
    Includes bibliographical references and index.
    ISBN 0-7658-0028-4 (alk. paper)
    1. Jewish philosophers—United States—Biography. 2. Jewish judges—United States—Biography. 3. United States. Supreme Court—Biography—History. 4. Rabbis—United States—Biography 5. Jews—United States—Intellectual life—20th century. 6. United States—Civilization—Jewish influences. 7. United States—Biogra-phy. I. Title.

E184.37 .A153 2000
973.04'924'0099—dc21   00-037388

For Mary

"Many waters cannot quench love,
neither can the floods drown it."

—Song of Songs

"Now let us go forward, whether we shall give
glory to another man, or he to us."

—Homer

Contents

Acknowledgments

Grateful acknowledgement is made to the following publishers or publications for permission to reprint essays in this book, as follows:

New York University Press for the essays on Horace M. Kallen and Morris Raphael Cohen from *The Other New York Jewish Intellectuals*, Carole S. Kessner, ed. (1994), and the essay on Jacob Agus from *American Rabbi: The Life and Thought of Jacob Agus*, Steven T. Katz, ed. (1996).

Prometheus Books for the essay on Sidney Hook from *Sidney Hook: Philosopher of Democracy and Humanism*, Paul Kurtz, ed. (1983).

B'nai B'rith for the essay on Louis D. Brandeis from *Great Jewish Personalities in Modern Times*, Simon Noveck, ed. (1960).

Theodor Herzl Foundation for the essay on Benjamin Nathan Cardozo that appeared in the May/June 1999 issue of *Midstream* and part of the essay on Leo Jung that appeared in the August/ September 1993 issue of the magazine.

American Jewish Congress for the essay on Robert Gordis that was published in *Judaism*, Winter 1993 issue.

Introduction

As the captives sat by the waters of Babylon, they asked, "How shall we sing the Lord's song in a foreign land?" In a score or more of centuries, by the waters of many lands, Jews have asked this question. In the twelfth century in Spain, Judah Halevi cried that though he lived in the West, his heart was in the East.

Today, as I write these words, a Jew is poet laureate of the United States, by appointment of the Library of Congress. As he sits by the waters of the Potomac, Robert Pinsky does not mourn that his heart is in the East and does not ask, "How shall I sing the Lord's song in a foreign land." Though he has not forgotten Jerusalem, with Walt Whitman he believes that the "United States themselves are essentially the greatest poem." How can the greatest poem not be the Lord's song?

The nine American Jews about whom I write in this book were not poets. They were philosophers, or jurists, or rabbis. They did not consider themselves captives sitting by the waters of Babylon, and though each of them, in his own private way, remembered Jerusalem, each in his own way sang the Lord's song and believed that the United States was the greatest poem, perhaps even the Lord's song.

Six of the persons about whom there are essays in this book are widely known and are readily accepted as American Jewish thinkers; namely, Horace M. Kallen, Morris Raphael Cohen, Louis D. Brandeis, Leo Jung, Robert Gordis, and Jacob B. Agus. One may, however, wonder how I have come to include essays on Sidney Hook, Justice Cardozo, and Justice Frankfurter, for they were not known in their lifetime to have made important contributions to Jewish life or thought. They are included because their work reflected essential Jewish values. Each in his own way dedicated his life to *tikun olam*, to the betterment of life and the advancement of human ideals. Justice Cardozo

1

and Justice Frankfurter each used his genius, his superior intellectual gifts in legal analysis and creative interpretation and insights in the interests of justice; and Sidney Hook applied his massive powers of intelligence, of reason and intellect, to the pursuit of truth and the enhancement of human liberty and righteousness.

The nine persons belong together as American thinkers. Their Americanism permeated all their thoughts. But how Jewish were they? This is a rather thorny question. If their Jewishness is defined by religion, then only the three rabbis and possibly Cardozo would qualify; the other five clearly belong in the nonreligious, or secularist, category. But I mention this differentiation only to brush it aside, for I see no great wall of separation that keeps apart the secularists from the religious Jews. In this complex world secularists often serve God more handsomely than do members of synagogues or temples. When the Supreme Court in 1954 (with Felix Frankfurter playing a key role behind the scenes) unanimously agreed to outlaw segregation of the races in public schools, was the Court's action secular or religious? When, in 1990, Congress passed the statute known as the Americans With Disabilities Act, that requires equality of treatment of handicapped persons, was the action secular or religious? Is a minimum wage act secular or religious? Is Medicaid a secular or a religious act? The lines of distinction are not merely blurred, they are no longer relevant. Horace Kallen wrote a book with the title *Secularism is the Will of God*. The title neatly summarizes a philosophy of religion, or a philosophy of secularism. For it is our religion that teaches us to transcend religion to do God's will.

The story is told of a pious Jew asking his rabbi: "We are taught that everything in life has its purpose but what possible use can be found in atheism?' "Ah!" said the rabbi; "atheism has a great purpose. For when you see a homeless man, you might say to him, not to worry, God will provide him with a home. Or when you see a man who is in need of food, you might say to him to wait for God will provide him with food. If you behave this way, you will he a great sinner. You must act as if there is no God. You must act as if you do not believe that God exists. You must provide shelter, you must provide food for the poor!"

A Jewish community that values its traditions has societies that are directed to meet every ethical obligation: it has a Hebrew free loan society, an organization that provides poor brides with dowries, a free clothing society, a house that is a shelter for indigent travelers, and so on and on, organizations set up to take care of needs from birth to burial (including a free burial society). For Judaism teaches that God exists in order to teach us how to act as if God did not exist!

The Talmud records that the ancient rabbis of Yavneh had a favorite saying: "I am a creature of God and my neighbor also is his creature. My work is in the city and his is in the field. I rise early to my work and he rises early to his. But perhaps you may say that I do great things and he does small things. We have learned that it matters not whether a man does much or little, if only he directs his heart to heaven" (Berachot 17a). It is in the spirit of the ancient rabbis that I obliterate the distinction between the religious and the secularists who are included in these essays.

In a Hebrew poem that he wrote in the mid-nineteenth century, Judah Leib Gordon wrote, "Be a Jew in your tent, and a human being when you go out." But this advice is based on the idea that Judaism or Jewishness can be confined to a limited sphere; that Jew and Mensch are radically different beings; that one can be a Jew and not be a Mensch. Socrates, it should be ever remembered, prayed that the outer and the inner man be at one. The ideal of Torah u-Madda, Torah and secular learning, Judaism and secularism, does not contemplate a bifurcation of the Jew, but an enlargement, so that one's secularism is religious, one's religion is secularist.

I want the reader to know that six of the essays--those about the three philosophers and those about the three rabbis--are about persons who were my dear friends. I make mention of the fact with natural pride and satisfaction. I believe that one is justified to have concerned himself with the life and thought of persons whom he liked and loved, whom he admired and respected.

The division of the book into three parts reflects my own intellectual and religious interests. Philosophy and Judaism, however, unlike the law, could not be compartmentalized. They permeated all my other interests. They possessed not only my mind but also my heart. Perhaps this is why the philosophers and the rabbis stood in a special relation to me. They spoke to me not only with their minds but also with their hearts, and demonstrated to me how a person can direct his heart to heaven.

Part 1

Philosophers

1

Horace M. Kallen

Horace Meyer Kallen (1882–1974) was—together with John Dewey, Charles Beard, Thorstein Veblen, and James Harvey Robinson—one of the founding faculty of the New School for Social Research when it was established in 1919, and he was there as a professor of philosophy and of social psychology for a full half-century. Even before he began to teach at the New School, Kallen achieved national attention for his writings on cultural pluralism as a national objective in place of the melting pot idea. He pioneered as a Zionist and influenced Justice Louis D. Brandeis in the formulation of a philosophy of American Zionism. He was an early participant in the work of the American Civil Liberties Union and of civil rights organizations, and was one of the first Americans to support and help formulate philosophies of consumerism, adult education, and, especially, Jewish education. His philosophy of individualism, of the right to be different, of pragmatism, and his idea of Hebraism have influenced many thinkers.

To celebrate the centenary of Kallen's birth, a conference was held at the New School, that was sponsored by the New School, the American Jewish Congress, and the American Section of the World Jewish Congress. The papers that were there presented, together with several others, have been published in *The Legacy of Horace M. Kallen*, edited by Milton R. Konvitz (Fairleigh Dickinson University Press and Herzl Press, 1987). See also Sidney Hook and Milton R. Konvitz, eds., *Freedom and Experience: Essays Presented to Horace M. Kallen* (Cornell University Press, 1947).

* * *

For about a half-century, Horace Kallen occupied a special—for many of these years, a unique—place on the Jewish scene in the United States. For he was not a professional Jew, not a rabbi, not a professor in a rabbinical seminary, not a scholar who made a specialty of Judaic study, not eminent among Jews by reason of the high office he held in a Jewish organization. He was the first Jewish professor of a non-Jewish subject in a non-Jewish college or university who was intimately and prominently identified with Jewish interests, Jewish concerns, Jewish organizations.[1] While widely recognized and honored as a thinker, philosopher, and psychologist, Kallen devoted much of his time and thought to Jewish problems and influenced Jewish educators, communal workers, rabbis, and Jewish public opinion. In some ways he served as a role model emulated by his peers and many younger men and women, who looked to him for guidance and direction. In all these respects Kallen had no predecessor, and, regrettably, no successor. In American Jewish history he carved out for himself a very special place. He was, by reason of that very special place, *primus inter omnes*.

Kallen was born on August 11, 1882, in Berenstadt, a town in the German province of Silesia (now Poland). His parents were Jacob David and Esther Rebecca (Glazier) Kallen. His father, who had emigrated from Latvia, studied at a yeshiva and was an assistant rabbi in Berenstadt. As a foreigner, Rabbi Kallen was expelled from Germany and emigrated to the United States. When Horace Kallen was five years old, his father returned to Berenstadt and moved his wife, Horace, who was the eldest child, and two daughters to the United States, where he became rabbi of an Orthodox congregation in Boston. Rabbi Kallen (the original family name was Kalonymous, the name of many medieval Jewish families) was a scholarly man; at the time of his death in 1917, he left some manuscripts that have remained unpublished. The son was close to his mother, who died in 1928, but was alienated from his father, whom he remembered as a domineering father and husband. For many years father and son were estranged, but when his father was on his deathbed, Horace Kallen sat beside him for a fortnight until he died. During those two weeks parent and son achieved a reconciliation, and on the wall of his study Professor Kallen had a framed photograph of both his parents.[2]

Rabbi Kallen apparently tried to keep his son from attending a public school and to teach him at home, but when the truant officer threatened Rabbi Kallen, he sent Horace to an elementary school. The boy also attended a heder for his Jewish studies; and after school he sold newspapers, to help support the large Kallen family, for in due course there were eight children. The father wanted the son to follow in his footsteps, but Horace rebelled and at times ran away from home. Professor Kallen remembered his years through elementary and secondary schools as very troublesome. The rebellion was not only against his father, but also against the father's religion. Although reconciled to his father in the latter's last days, he did not sit shiva nor say Kaddish for him. His estrangement from Judaism as a religion was never overcome.

When he was eighteen years old, Kallen entered Harvard College, and in 1903, received his B.A. *magna cum laude*. His years as an undergraduate were perhaps the most important for his intellectual and spiritual development. His interest in philosophy, however, had started while he had been still living at home, where one day he discovered among his father's books a copy of Spinoza's *Ethics* and the *Tractatus Theologico-Politicus* in a German translation. These books excited his eager mind. As a freshman at Harvard he took a philosophy course with Santayana, and as a junior, a course with William James. James especially influenced him; both the person and his teaching had a lifelong impact on Kallen.

In addition to William James, another Harvard professor greatly influenced Kallen. That was Barrett Wendell, whose field was American literary history. Kallen took a course with Professor Wendell in his sophomore year, a course in which Wendell tried to expose and evaluate the Hebraic elements in American literary and political thought and institutions. Kallen tried to close his mind against this teaching but in private conversations with his argumentative student the professor won out, and Kallen began consciously and eagerly to reclaim and to identify himself with his Jewish background and inheritance, with Jewish culture, and with the Jewish people. He continued, however, to reject Judaism as a religion. This was the beginning of Kallen's commitment to agnosticism, Jewish secularism, Jewish culture, Zionism, Hebraism, cultural pluralism.

After graduating from Harvard, Kallen became an instructor in English at Princeton, where he remained for two years. When his contract was not renewed, it was intimated that had it been known he was a Jew, he would not have been appointed in the first place.[3] He then returned to Harvard as a graduate student and wrote his Ph.D. dissertation under the direction of William James. He received his degree in 1908, and remained at Harvard for the following three years as a lecturer and teaching assistant to James, Santayana, and Josiah Royce, the three philosophical giants who made Harvard's philosophy department world-famous. During this period Kallen in 1907 received a Sheldon fellowship that made it possible for him to travel to Europe, where he studied under F. C. S. Schiller, noted pragmatist at Oxford, and attended the lectures of Henri Bergson in Paris. Kallen then taught philosophy and psychology at the University of Wisconsin from 1911 to 1918, but resigned over an issue of academic freedom. During his years at Wisconsin, Kallen published three books: a study of James and Bergson, *The Structure of Lasting Peace*, and the book that has had the longest life, *The Book of Job as a Greek Tragedy*, published in 1918. It was in those years, too, that Kallen published his articles in the *Nation* (in 1915) that represented the first formulation of his philosophy of cultural pluralism, and it was in those years, too, that he became involved in Zionist thought and affairs.

In 1919, as the New School for Social Research was being established in New York, Kallen was invited to become a member of the founding faculty, joining Alvin Johnson, John Dewey, James Harvey Robinson, Thorstein Veblen, and other famous scholars. He readily accepted the invitation and remained at the New School for over a half-century.

Kallen was not cast in the mold of a conventional philosopher. He was too greatly interested in political and economic movements, in civil liberties and civil rights, in the labor movement, in the consumers' cooperative movement, to allow himself to become completely absorbed in the life of a detached, self-isolated thinker.[4] High among his interests were Zionism, Jewish education, adult education, Jewish culture, pragmatism, the philosophy of pluralism, art and aesthetics—indeed, of Kallen it may be truly said that nothing human, no human concern, was alien to him. The institutions that he helped found or that he supported to his last day—the American Jewish Congress, the American Association for Jewish Education (which later became the Jewish Education Service of North America), the Jewish Teachers Seminary—Herzliah, the Farband Labor Zionist Order (later the Labor Zionist Alliance), the Rochdale Institute, the New School for Social Research—were for Kallen sacred treasures, and this showed where his heart lay.

Who were the persons who had influenced Kallen? In 1935 he wrote that the paramount influences were William James, George Santayana, Barrett Wendell, F. C. S. Schiller, Edwin B. Holt,[5] and Solomon Schechter. In later years he added John Dewey, Louis D. Brandeis, and Edward Everett Hale.[6] On the walls of his study at home were portraits of Goethe, Jefferson, William James, Santayana, John Dewey, Hale, Judge Julian Mack,[7] and Solomon Schechter, in addition to the photograph of his parents.

As we have said, when Horace Kallen enrolled as a freshman at Harvard College, his feelings towards Judaism and Jewishness were more than negative, they were feelings of hostility, of total rejection. But Professor Barrett Wendell "converted" him to Judaism—albeit not to the religion of his father, Rabbi Kallen, but to the heritage of Jewish culture, thought, and values, to a positive feeling of membership in the Jewish people, an openness to being Jewish and to the Jewish experience. Like Heine, Kallen felt as if he had never really left the Jewish community and that his "conversion" was only a restoration of his sight.

Before long, Kallen discovered Zionism and threw himself into Zionist activity. In 1902 Solomon Schechter came to the United States to become head of the Jewish Theological Seminary, and soon after meeting Schechter, young Horace Kallen came to think of him as his "revered friend and teacher." Three years after his arrival in the United States, Schechter stated that Zionism was a great bulwark against assimilation; he supported religious and spiritual-cultural Zionism, and despite opposition from leading members of the board of trustees of the Seminary, he opened the institution to Zionism and attended the eleventh Zionist Congress in Vienna.

To understand Kallen's early and lifelong devotion to Zionism, it is necessary to see it in the context of his broader philosophical stance, of which Zionism was, for him, a prime example and the application of his philosophy to his own life and his own living values. And so we shall at this point consider his philosophy of cultural pluralism.

In his first formulation of cultural pluralism, in 1915[8] Kallen had in mind only the ethnic groups to which Americans belonged, and he thought of this membership as something which the individual could not easily shed. The ethnic group was a *Gemeinschaft*,[9] a natural, not a voluntary, community. While a person could cease to be a citizen or a member of a church, or cease to be a carpenter or a lawyer, he could not cease to be a Jew or a Pole. A man, he wrote, cannot change his grandfather. Later, however, Kallen came to think that while a person cannot change his or her grandparents, he or she can, indeed, reject them—as many have done.[10] All associations, he thought, ought to be voluntary: a person ought to be able to reject the fact that he or she is a Jew or a Pole—that membership in a group should be by "contract" and not by "status."[11] But Kallen continued to believe that participation in one's ethnic group and in its special culture has great significance for a person's self-identity, sense of worth and dignity, and for the person's full human development.

While Kallen held fast to a belief in individualism, he contended that no individual is merely an individual. "States, churches, industries, families are organizations, not organisms," he wrote, and added:

> They are associations of men ant women occurring not because they inwardly must, but because an outward condition calls for control or manipulation which individuals cannot accomplish alone. There are no social institutions which are primary, which are ends in themselves, as individuals are ends in themselves.[12]

The elemental term in every union, in every association, wrote Kallen, is "the individual, in his indefeasible singularity."

Although Kallen held fast to this belief in individualism, he was ready to admit that, he said,

> he knew of no instance ... of an individual building his personal history solely by himself, from himself, on himself; feeding, so to speak, on nothing but his own flesh ant spirit and growing by what he feeds on.[13]

Kallen's individualism was not, therefore, "rugged individualism," not narcissistic or solipsistic; rugged individualism was only a case of extreme selfishness; when invoked as an ideal, it can only defeat defensible individualism. For inherent in individualism, as understood by Kallen, is the principle of cooperation—but cooperation that is voluntary, cooperation that does not replace the primacy of the individual with the primacy of the state or society.

In 1909 Israel Zangwill's *The Melting Pot* was published, and the play had a long run on Broadway. Its theme—later rejected by Zangwill himself—was that "America is God's crucible, the great melting-pot where all the races of Europe are melting and reforming." The melting-pot idea was the pervasive, dominant view of the Protestant establishment. Immigrants were expected to shed their religious and cultural baggage at Ellis Island or as soon after their arrival as possible. This was the meaning of the "Americanization" process. Jews who had settled in the United States in the nineteenth century accepted this conception of what the American Idea intended. Jews and all other immigrants were to become "assimilated," homogenized. To them any other way meant segregation, and segregation meant that the ghetto would be transferred to America—a dangerous and repulsive idea.

It was against this ideological background that Kallen promulgated the idea of cultural pluralism and his version of the American Idea. Kallen rejected both assimilation and segregation, and pointed to the Declaration of Independence, the Constitution, the Emancipation Proclamation, Lincoln's Second Inaugural Address, Washington's Farewell Address, and Jefferson's First Inaugural as the basic documents expressing the American Idea,[14] the essence of which is that the purpose of freedom is to guarantee the right to be different—not to abolish differences, but to sustain and enhance them. But different individuals, and the different groups that they compose, are not to isolate themselves but to cooperate one with another. Differences were to be "orchestrated." The motto "E pluribus unum" does not mean just "unum," just oneness (the melting-pot idea), nor does it mean just "pluribus," each individual and each group, each ethnic or racial or religious group, each culture, existing separately, rigidly segregated. No, the ideal means that the diversity exists but all the diversities are a union, just as an orchestra is a union of diversities.[15]

Kallen gave this conception of cultural pluralism or the American Idea many different expressions. This is how he expressed it in an essay in 1942:

> In affirming that *all* men are created equal, and that the rights of *all* to life, liberty and the pursuit of happiness are *unalienable*, it [the Declaration of Independence] accepts human beings as they are, with all the variety and multiplicity of faith, of race, of sex, of occupations, of ideas, of possessions; and it affirms the equal right of these different people freely to struggle for existence and for growth in freedom and in happiness as different.... The American way of life, then, may be said to flow from each man's unalienable right to be different...[16]

This understanding of the American Idea, said Kallen, translates in the political order as equal suffrage, and as government by the people and for the people—all people; in the economic order it means free enterprise; in religion, freedom of conscience; in the arts and sciences, freedom of inquiry, of research, of expression. It means freedom of association into sects, parties, corporations, trade unions, fraternal orders, and many other voluntary associations.[17]

Now, the national being rests upon the cooperative and competitive relationships of these diverse voluntary associations. And the members of these associations have each of them multiple associations. A member of the Bar, for example, is at the same time a citizen, a family member, a member of a church or synagogue, member of a political party, a social club, an alumni association, and so forth.

> Each [membership] is a different way of his being together with other people. He is the bond which unites the societies with one another.... His relations are not fixed by status; they are not coerced, ... but are liquid and mobile. This mobility of relationships is what gives its characteristic quality to the national living. Of this quality [of national living] the consummation is Cultural Pluralism. For its diverse and ever-diversifying members are united with one another in and through their differences, and the singularity of our culture is the orchestration of those manifold differences—e pluribus unum—into the common faith...[18]

Throughout his many years, Kallen applied, and kept on applying, the fact and ideal of cultural pluralism to American Jewry. He saw American Jews as constituting a group that, in the mix that is the American nation, is

> one more variety in the dynamic whole, is, like the addition of another taste or sight or sound, an enrichment, a contribution to abundance, spiritual and material. If against the assimilationist the American spirit affirms the right to be different, against the segregationist it affirms the right of free association of the different with one another.[19]

In addition, the Jewish group has a special claim of priority, for, Kallen noted, the American community was established through the Hebrew Scriptures, a fact that contributes heavily to "the singularity of the Jewish psyche," and he quoted the judgment of the historian William E. H. Lecky that "the Hebraic mortar cemented the foundations of American democracy." And Kallen added one more attribution: that the Jewish community, as every other composing the American nation, "serves as a psychological locale for voluntary social experimentation, for invention and discovery, [and] as such involving more limited risks than a national-wide adventure would. " In this way American Jewry has made its contribution to employer-employee relations, to philanthropy, to education, to literature and the arts. Such and other contributions represent both an Americanization of Jews and also an enrichment of the American way: thus "American Jewish living" is in a healthy symbiotic relationship with all other forms of living, "whose interaction orchestrates the Union we call America, and whose combined utterance is the American spirit."[20]

This philosophy of cultural pluralism as applied specifically to American Jews can be valid, said Kallen,

> only for those Americans whose faith in democracy is a fighting faith, and for those American Jews who are resolved to stand up in the armies of democracy as the democratic faith requires, freely and boldly as Jews.[21]

As we have noted, Kallen agreed with Lecky that "the Hebraic mortar cemented the foundations of American democracy." What is Hebraism? In an essay written as early as 1909,[22] Kallen contrasted Hellenism and Hebraism. For the Greeks, he wrote, the essence of reality was an order that was immutable and eternal. For the Greek mind, change was unreal and evil; the universe was static. Hebraism, on the contrary, saw reality as flux, change, dynamic and functional. Kallen thought that the Book of Job was the most representative book of Hebraism, and he never tired of quoting from it the cry of Job: "I know that He will slay me; nevertheless will I maintain my ways before Him." In his commentary on this cry Kallen tried to encapsulate the essence of the Hebraic Idea:

> The very act of maintaining one's ways may render the slaying impossible. To believe in life in the face of death, to believe in goodness in the face of evil, to hope for better times to come, to work at bringing them about—that is Hebraism. Whether Biblical or Talmudic, that is the inner history of Jews, from the beginning to the present day—an optimistic struggle against overwhelming odds. That is Hebraism, but it is the Hebraism, not of childhood and innocence; it is the Hebraism of old age and experience. It is a vision of the world that has been tested in the furnace and [has] come out clean.[23]

Kallen saw Hebraism in the philosophy of William James, whose pragmatism defined an idea or thing by what it does. Ideas are true if they lead to successful fruition, if they endure, if they have survival value. And Kallen saw in Bergson "the most adequate exponent" of a "tested and purified philosophic Hebraism." For Bergson change and not immutability was real, and such a finding, in which the dynamic, and not the static, is real, was for Kallen "the essential finding of Hebraism."[24]

In his writing early in the twentieth century Kallen attacked Reform Judaism for denying the particularity of Judaism and stressing its universal elements and teachings, for, he contended, "Particularity, as opposed to universality, is the essence of life and power. The most universal thing is the deadest.... Hebraism is a life and not a tradition; ... a concrete and particular mode of behavior, not a formula." Hebraism and Judaism are not "dead unalterable 'universals.' " Contending against the early leaders of Reform Judaism, Kallen maintained that "What really destroys the Jews is what 'universalizes' them, what empties their life of distinctive particular content and substitutes void phrases to be filled with any meaning the social and religious fashion of the day casts up." Because it is particularistic, individualistic, and not universalistic in its basic metaphysical and general philosophical forces and tendencies, the essence of Hebraism is plastic and fluid, and so compatible with science and accommodating "to every pressing human need."[25]

This particularism, as it relates to the Jewish people, Kallen, early in his life, translated into Zionism. In an article published in 1910 Kallen wrote, "I am a Zionist." And he elaborated: "I look toward the concentration and renationalization of the Jews." "I am committed," he wrote, "to the persistence of a 'Jewish separation' that shall be national, positive, dynamic and adequate."[26]

Within the context of his concern with Hebraism and Zionism, Kallen contended that eighteenth-century liberalism had overstressed and exaggerated the idea of the isolated individual; that liberalism had failed to see that individuality is not attained at birth but is something that one needs to achieve; that all persons in their beginning depend on a society. Genuine liberalism, he argued, requires for the group, for the races and nationalities, the same freedom of development and expression as that required for the individual. Indeed, insofar as this freedom is required for the individual, it must be required for the group, for races and nations are "the essential reservoirs of individuality."

Through national freedom, the Jewish people would be able to render service to mankind, and for this the Jewish people need to have their national home in Palestine. The Jew, Kallen contended, will not win emancipation as a human being, as an individual, unless he first wins it as a Jew, and "the prerequisite to liberation of the individual is the liberation of the group to which he by birth belongs." Thus Zionism demands "not only group autonomy, but complete individual liberty for the Jew *as* Jew."[27] Enlightenment failed the Jew because it offered him liberty as an individual provided he ceased being a Jew. Zionism corrects this misconceived proposal; it offers the Jew complete individual liberty, not as an abstract human being, but as a Jew. While the Enlightenment offered to remove all inferiorities, it also removed all differences. The Enlightenment was, thus, a kind of melting pot; it was based on the misconception that equality had to mean identity or similarity. It failed to recognize the idea that there can be equality based on the right to be different.

It should be apparent that all the essential ingredients of what came to be known as cultural pluralism were already the constituents of what Kallen called Hebraism and what he had recognized as Zionism. On the published record, it seems that Kallen had arrived at cultural pluralism through his thinking about himself as a Jew and what meaning and significance his Jewishness should have for him. It was in an essay on "Judaism, Hebraism, Zionism," published in 1910, that Kallen wrote:

> Culture ... constitutes a harmony, of which peoples and nations are the producing instruments, to which each contributes its unique tone, in which the whole human past is present as an enduring tension, as a background from which the present comes to light and draws its character, color, vitality.[28]

Here one sees the metaphor of the orchestra, the harmony that was the orchestration of differences.

Thus it was that, by some invisible complex process, there fused in Horace Kallen's mind ideas that had made their way into it from the Hebrew Scriptures, from William James, Barrett Wendell, Louis Brandeis, Herzl, Moses Hess, Thomas Jefferson, James Madison, Solomon Schechter, Henri Bergson, Thomas Paine, and Ralph Waldo Emerson—strange bedfellows; yet in his mind all were on friendly speaking terms, so that they all became harmoniously orchestrated; they came in separately but came out as cultural pluralism, as the American Idea, as Hebraism, as Zionism. Kallen could have said, quoting from T. S. Eliot's "East Coker,": "In my beginning is my end."

Reflecting upon his own intellectual development, in 1933 Kallen wrote: "It is upon the foundation and against the background of my Jewish cultural milieu that my vision of America was grown." It is not that he saw Zionism through his vision of America; the order was the reverse: he saw America through his vision of Hebraism, Zionism. He read the Declaration of Independence against his memory of the emancipation of the Israelites from Egyptian slavery. In the parental Kallen household, he wrote,

> the suffering and slavery of Israel were commonplaces of conversation; from Passover to Passover, freedom was an ideal ceremonially reverenced, religiously aspired to. The textbook story of the Declaration of Independence came upon me, nurtured upon the deliverance from Egypt and the bondage in exile, like the clangor of trumpets, like a sudden light. What a recounting battle cry of freedom![29]

Zionism to Kallen did not, however, mean the negation of the Diaspora. He wanted Jewish life and Jewish ideals to flourish and flower in America no less than in Israel. And the key to the future of a Jewish life, wherever Jews made their home, is Jewish education. For the last forty years of his life Kallen, therefore, worked closely with leading Jewish educators, with Samson Benderly, Ben Rosen, I. B. Berkson, Israel S. Chipkin, Alexander M. Dushkin, Judah Pilch, Oscar Janowsky, A. P. Schoolman, and Emanuel Gamoran. He attended countless meetings and conferences, traveling everywhere to lecture and exhort on behalf of Jewish education. At times it appeared as if it was his life's mission. And whenever an opportunity presented itself, he tried to explain what teaching the Jewish tradition should mean and be. He did not mean that Jewish schools should teach the history and thought of the Jewish past as the pastness of the past. No, tradition is a process, an ongoing activity, and activity in the present changes the past. A person or group *makes* his or her or its past, and so the past is constantly remade, and in this way the tradition becomes a *living* tradition. Thus the Bible can be a part of my past, a part of my tradition, only because it is a part of my *present* life.

Kallen never tired of teaching this lesson; he formulated it in countless ways. A typical statement is the following from a book published in 1956:

> The word [tradition] means, literally, carrying on, a continuous ongoing—but a carrying on, or ongoing, as any person's life goes on, not changelessly, but as a process of changing, where the old phases both continue in the new and are altered by the new. Self-preservation, whether of an individual or a group, is this process wherein the past ensures only as it lives on in the present and future, and lives on only as it is changed by them.[30]

People say they cannot change the past. But Kallen would ask: "What else is there to change? What else is the present but the past changing?" "A living culture is a changing culture."

It should be noted that Kallen did not view Hebraism as an isolated phenomenon. In the United States Hebraism is to be a part of Americanism. The Jew is to be a Jewish American person. In an essay written in 1955, Kallen explained the union or fusion or interplay as follows:

> Such consummations are beyond the reach of the individual isolate and alone. They require a home-centered community with its traditions of language, diet, worship, feasting and fasting, play and sport, expressive and representative arts, all carrying forward communal remembrance, beliefs, works and ways.... Their communication by the generations is what sustains the communion which holds the altering community together. They are what Jewish in Jewish American signifies. They thrive best when supported by a free trade with their peers of different communal cultures, assimilating and hence transfiguring what they get in exchange, and again communicating the new life-form of their changing and growing old culture to their non-Jewish neighbors, and receiving theirs in return. The social orchestration which this intercultural exchange consummates actualizes the American Idea and gives the culture of the American people the qualities that Whitman and Emerson and William James and Louis Brandeis celebrated.[31]

Horace Kallen referred to himself as a humanist, a temporalist, a pragmatist, an instrumentalist, and to his philosophy as Cultural Pluralism, Hebraism, as the Hebraic Idea, as the American Idea. Perhaps all these terms ought to be strung together, linked by hyphens. "The hyphen," he wrote, "unites very much more than it separates."[32] Kallen was perhaps the most hyphenated American thinker, and so he lived more abundantly, more richly, more freely, and to whomsoever and whatsoever he was linked he gave abundantly, richly, freely. That his influence is lasting is borne out by the fact that in 1990, some sixteen years after his death in 1974, seventeen of Kallen's books were in print.

In the last quarter of the twentieth century, however, both the melting-pot idea and cultural pluralism were under attack from forces that preached and practiced "otherness"—not assimilation, not pluralism, but ethnicity; that ethnic, racial, and cultural differences are not bridgeable. And this reactionary ideology has worldwide ramifications, for everywhere there is a recrudesence of tribalism, regional chauvinism, and blazing nationalism. One cannot foresee when, if ever, these forces will have dissipated their strength. Meanwhile, there is a struggle between the children of light and the children of darkness; but struggle, Horace Kallen taught, is an indispensable quality of all life, human no less than animal—we struggle, he wrote, if only so that we may go on struggling, for that is life.

Notes

1. Morris Raphael Cohen came on the Jewish scene, as an activist Jew, some twenty to twenty-five years after Kallen.
2. The biographical facts are based on a long interview with Kallen by me and the late Dorothy Kuhn (Mrs. Adolph S.) Oko, in August 1964, at Truro, Mass. The interview was later made part of the oral history collection of the American Jewish Committee. The biographical facts are also based on many conversations and on an extensive correspondence between Kallen and the author. The interview and correspondence are at the Documentation Center, School of Industrial and Labor Relations, Cornell University, Ithaca, N.Y.
3. Cf. Ludwig Lewisohn, *Upstream: An American Chronicle* (New York: Boni & Liveright. 1922).
4. See Sidney Hook and M. R. Konvitz, eds., *Freedom and Experience: Essays Presented to Horace M. Kallen* (Ithaca, N.Y.: Cornell University Press, 1947), Preface, viii.
5. *Edwin B. Halt was an American psychologist, author of The* Concept of Consciousness (1914), *The Freudian Wish* (1915), and other works.
6. Edward Everett Hale was the son of Nathan Hale and nephew of Edward Everett; a Unitarian clergyman. author of the famous short story, "The Man without a Country," and active in civil improvement and philanthropic work.
7. Julian W. Mack (1866–1943), from 1913, to his retirement in 1941, was judge of the U.S. Court of Appeals; a pioneer in work on behalf of child welfare and on the problem of juvenile delinquency; a Zionist leader, president of the Zionist Organization of America and president of the first American Jewish Congress in 1918; and a member of the Harvard University Board of Overseers for eighteen years.
8. "Democracy versus the Melting Pot." *Nation* 100 (Feb. 18, 25, 1915): 190-94, 217-20. Reprinted in *Culture and Democracy: Studies in the Group Psychology of the American Peoples* (New York: Boni & Liveright, 1924), hereinafter referred to as *Culture and Democracy*.
9. Cf. Ferdinand Tönnies, *Gemeinschaft und Gesellschaft* (1887).
10. *Culture and Democracy*, 94, 122, 123.
11. Cf. Sir Henry Maine, *Ancient Law* (1861).
12. *Individualism, an American Way of Life* (New York: Liveright, 1933), 142.
13. *Culture and Democracy*, 181.
14. Kallen, "The National Being and the Jewish Community," in Oscar I. Janowsky, ed., *The American Jew: A Composite Portrait* (New York: Harper & Bros., 1942), 270, at 277.
15. Ibid., 280.
16. Ibid., 278.
17. Ibid., 279.
18. Ibid., 280-81.
19. Ibid., 283.

20. Ibid., 284.
21. Ibid., 285.
22. The essay is reprinted in Kallen, *Judaism at Bay* (New York: Bloch Publishing, 1932).
23. Ibid., 13.
24. Ibid., 14.
25. Ibid., 39.
26. Ibid., 33.
27. Ibid., 116.
28. Ibid., 37.
29. Ibid., 7.
30. Kallen, *Cultural Pluralism and the American Idea* (Philadelphia: University of Pennsylvania Press, 1956), 23.
31. *Jewish Social Service Quarterly* 32 (Fall 1955): 27.
32. *Culture and Democracy*, 63.

2

Morris Raphael Cohen

Morris Raphael Cohen (1880-1947) was a leading American philosopher. He taught philosophy at the City College of New York from 1912 to 1938. His teaching was famous for the Socratic irony that provoked an interest in philosophy and the scientific method; his teaching and his books influenced his best students, some of whom themselves became famous philosophers. His first book, *Reason and Nature: An Essay on the Meaning of Scientific Method*, was published in 1931 when Cohen was fifty-one years old. He published three other books before his death, and then nine additional books were published posthumously, including *The Meaning of Human History* (1947), which Cohen considered his magnum opus. Although an agnostic, he was deeply devoted to study of the Hebrew Bible and Jewish thought and history. In 1933 he founded the Conference on Jewish Relations; together with Professor Salo W. Baron, he founded and edited the quarterly *Jewish Social Studies*; after his retirement he devoted most of his time to Jewish interests. His substantial contributions to jurisprudence and the philosophy of law were recognized by a distinguished symposium at the Hebrew University in Jerusalem that marked the centennial of his birth; the papers were published in the *Israel Law Review* (vol. 16, July 1981). See also Salo W. Baron, Ernest Nagel, and Koppel S. Pinson, eds. in *Reason and Freedom: Studies in Philosophy and Jewish Culture in Memory of Morris Raphael Cohen* (1951).

*　　*　　*

I

Morris Raphael Cohen and Horace M. Kallen were, I submit, the two most intensely Jewish thinkers, not only of their time, but also in the entire sweep of American history. One difference between them is that Kallen began his Jewish activity early in life and early in the twentieth century, while Cohen, two years his senior, began his Jewish activity in the early 1930s. Each of them was a professor of philosophy in a non-Jewish institution of higher learning at a time when very few Jews had appointments on college or university faculties, and each of them identified himself with Jewish interests and causes. The American Jewish community recognized in each of them great symbolic value as Jewish intellectuals who had won recognition as equals among American thinkers.[1] Each of them was a nonconventional, nontraditional philosopher, for, instead of concentrating on metaphysics and epistemology, they devoted their genius to the contributions that critical thinking can make to individual and social problems in law, science, politics, ethics, international relations, religion, ethnicity, and other matters that tangibly affect the lives, sufferings, and hopes of peoples and nations.

Cohen was born on July 25, 1880, at Minsk, chief city of Byelorussia. His father made a poor living as a presser. His parents were Orthodox, observant Jews, after they settled in New York, as they had been in Russia. In 1935 Cohen wrote about his father:

> "In all I knew of my father he conformed to the old conception of a saint. He was kindly, sympathetic, just in all his dealings, and never harming anyone, pained at the presence of any injustice or inequities, and always hoping for the triumph of good causes.[2]

Of his mother, Cohen wrote that she was the faithful and devoted companion of her husband for sixty-seven years, that she had a remarkable and vigorous intelligence, and that all the dreams of his life, that all the long communing with himself, were directly or indirectly connected with her and were endowed with some of her tenacious vitality.[3]

It was his maternal grandfather, however, who most profoundly influenced his early life. Between the ages of seven and ten Cohen lived with him in the city of Nesvizh, a city in Byelorussia where Isaac Elhanan (Spektor) was rabbi and where Rabbi Josef Baer

Soloveitchik was born, as was also Solomon Maimon, a city with a yeshiva, a Hebrew school, a kindergarten, a Yiddish school, and a Zionist social club. His grandfather was a tailor with a modest Jewish education.

During those three years Cohen attended a *heder* (or religious school) six days a week, generally from eight o'clock in the morning until after six, and yet, he remarked, his main education came from his grandfather. It was from his lips that he first heard the name Aristotle, and the name Maimonides (Rambam), and of Napoleon's campaign in Russia. It was in his grandfather's home that Cohen found a copy of a Hebrew version of Josephus, which he "devoured" and which gave him a taste for history that he never lost. Without the three years with his grandfather, Cohen wrote, "I could not have acquired the moral and intellectual interests which have been controlling in the course of my subsequent life." Years later, Cohen remarked that his grandfather's ascetic life had influenced his temperament "even more than my philosophy." On the day in 1890 when he was to take the train back to his parents in Minsk, Cohen wrote many years later,

> I was awakened by my grandfather kissing me good-bye. I was overcome with keen anguish that never, never would I see him again. The tears rolled down my cheeks before I knew it. Compared to my mother, he had been a hard taskmaster. But he had been the center of my life during three formative years of young boyhood and I realized even then, as I have more fully since, that he had laid the foundation not only of my intellectual development, but of that inner superiority to worldly fortune which is the essence of genuine nobility, spirituality, or as I prefer to call it now, the truly philosophic life.

It was walks and talks with his grandfather in Nesvizh that first stimulated Cohen's imagination about the world and history, that "gave a special zest to reflections on law and ethics which form the substance of Orthodox Hebrew education. His talks to me about Maimonides and the Book of Cusari [by Judah Halevi] stimulated an interest in the philosophy of religion that has never waned."[5] He returned to his parents' home in Minsk, where he remained for the following two years. In the Hebrew schools that he attended, in Minsk and in Nesvish, he studied Bible with Rashi's commentary, and Talmud, especially the Tractates Baba Kama and Gittin. His study at the *heder* was supplemented by study with a tutor engaged by his mother. Years later he wrote that "the Talmud had been my first teacher."[6]

In 1912 his family immigrated to the United States. His father had made the crossing of the Atlantic alone several times before in efforts to save enough money to take his family with him. The father came the first time to New York with a bundle containing his talit, tephilin (prayer shawl and phylacteries), and some underwear, and with 85 cents in his pocket, and he had no one awaiting him; no relative, no friend.[7] Years later Morris Cohen wrote of his parents, immigrants in a strange land, as persons "who were of that heroic generation that tore up their roots in their old homeland, and unaided and with no equipment other than their indomitable faith and courage, built new homes in this land and raised up children who have made invaluable contributions to the life of this country."[8]

II

The family moved into a three-room apartment on the corner of Broome and Norfolk Streets on the Lower East Side of Manhattan. Life was difficult, the father worked as a presser when employment was available, Morris Cohen tried to help out with after-school jobs selling newspapers or working at a soda fountain appurtenant to a poolroom operated by his brother. He was always eager, he wrote, "to lighten the burdens of my parents."[9] He once wrote that he would have liked to have lived over again the first fourteen years of his life, that in his fourteenth year he had "gained consciousness."[10] He read avidly; in 1897 he made a list of seventy-three cloth-bound and seventy-seven paperback books that he had read. While still in his 'teens he read extensively in history, including Gibbon, Mommsen, Green's *History of the English People*, Milman's *Notes on Roman History*, Freeman's *Ten Great Religions*, Marcus Aurelius, Ibsen, *Imitation of Christ*; the textbook that influenced him most, he wrote, was Meyer's *General History*, but it was Gibbon that made a more enduring impression on his thinking than any of the books he read in his courses. During that seedtime he thought that he would like to become a teacher or a journalist.[11]

In September 1895 he entered City College, from which he was graduated with the B. S. degree in 1900. He took courses in French and German, history, English, zoology, logic, and mathematics. He was especially impressed with the course in French literature, with the poetry of Racine and Corneille, with Moliere, Voltaire, and Victor

Hugo; he read John Stuart Mill's *Logic*, and books by Comte, Herbert Spencer, and George Herbert Palmer. He had not abandoned his interest in Jewish history and religion--he read Graetz's *History of the Jews*, and books on the higher criticism of the Bible. He read histories of Egypt and of Assyria and Babylonia. He was especially interested in pre-Socratic philosophy, and read Plato's *Parmenides* and Aristotle's *Metaphysics*, as well as Hegel's *Encyklopädie*.[12]

During his years as an upper-classman at CUNY, however, Cohen's chief intellectual interests were centered at the Educational Alliance on the Lower East Side more than at his college. In 1889 a number of Jewish cultural agencies amalgamated and formed the Hebrew Institute. Four years later the name was changed to Educational Alliance, of which Isidore Straus was president. Its Aguilar Free Library and reading room were stacked with Yiddish, Hebrew, English and Russian books and periodicals. The lectures offered there by Sholom Aleichem, Zvi Hirsch Masliansky, and other well-known literary and religious speakers attracted as many as 37,000 persons a week. There were English language classes, naturalization courses, preschool classes, literary and civic clubs, music and drama classes, art exhibits and a children's' orchestra. There was also a synagogue and a religious school.[13] Cohen started to resort to the Aguilar Free Library as soon as he learned to read English. But when he was eighteen years of age he discovered at the Educational Alliance a person who was to have a decisive influence on his life and thought, Thomas Davidson.

Davidson, identified as a philosopher and wandering scholar, was born in Scotland in 1840. In 1866 he came to Canada, and taught school in Toronto; then he came to St. Louis, wandered off to Boston, and at last came to New York and attached himself to the Educational Alliance. In a book about him published seven years after his death, he is described as follows:

> His learning was encyclopedic, and his culture almost universal. A great linguist, he had knowledge of philosophy in all its branches that was amazing.... But he was so humble and altruistic that very few of his friends and acquaintances knew what treasures were stored within his brain and heart. More than any of the nineteenth century thinkers known to fame, he lived and toiled for other people, and from first to last had no thought of himself.[14]

As we shall see, Cohen readily agreed with this estimate of the man. Davidson lived modestly and made his meager living by private teaching, tutoring, lecturing, and writing. He spent more than half of each year in leisurely study and frequent long visits in Europe. In London, he established the Fellowship of the New Life, of which the Fabian Society was an offshoot. In the fall of 1898 Davidson conducted a class at the Educational Alliance on Saturday evenings. With some misgivings and hesitation, Cohen started to attend these lectures and found them to be, to his amazement, interesting. After one of the sessions Davidson met Cohen and said to him: "You have a fine mind. You ought to cultivate it." "It was," Cohen later wrote, "years since anyone had paid me such a compliment." It was not long before Cohen thought of Davidson as his beloved teacher, and the teacher thought of Cohen as his son whom he would have liked to adopt. In his autobiography, Cohen wrote:

> "To me, as a youth of nineteen, Davidson had been a father, a guide into fields where he thought my highest possibilities lay, and an inspirer of efforts which became my life's passion.... None of us who were touched by his spirit can ever forget his heroic devotion to the pursuit and expression of truth as he saw it, in scorn of consequences or his magnificent disdain for worldly goods whenever he might serve the spiritual needs of those with whom he came into contact. None of us can ever forget the teacher who showed us that there are values of character, which remain when all else decays and that theirs are the enduring victory."[15]

It was Davidson who made Cohen study Latin, and who directed him to reading Hume's *Treatise on Human Nature* and Kant's *Critique of Pure Reason*. Is it any wonder that when Cohen was sixty-three years of age he referred to Davidson as one who had been "a light of my life and of my intellectual development"? Davidson also introduced Cohen to Tennyson, Dante, and Goethe, in each of whom Cohen maintained an interest to the end of his life. In 1889 Davidson bought a farm near Keene in the Adirondacks, where he spent eight months of the year (the four months December-March he was in New York at the Educational Alliance). He called his place Glenmore, and in the summers of 1889 and 1900 he there conducted a school of philosophy that attracted Stephen S. Wise, William James, John Dewey, Felix Adler, W. T. Harris (leading American Hegelian philosopher), and other scholars and thinkers. Davidson invited Cohen to come as his guest, and there Cohen met and established friendships with persons who were significant for his intellectual life. In the fall of 1900 Davidson was operated on for cancer and died at the age of sixty. Nine years after Davidson's death, Cohen wrote: "Davidson got hold of me when my soul was parched and all its zest for life gone. Through his personal friendship he opened the wells of life within me....the remembrance of my personal relation with him is enough to bear me up for a lifetime."[17] The extent and depth of Davidson's significance to Cohen may in part be measured by the fact that Cohen made annual pilgrimages to Davidson's grave at Glenmore ; the last such visit was in August 1941, when Cohen was sixty-one years of age.[18]

One additional important fact with respect to the Davidson-Cohen relationship needs to be mentioned. Immediately after Davidson's death, Cohen and other young students who had been attached to him decided that it was imperative that the work that Davidson had started at the Educational Alliance ought to be continued. They therefore established the Breadwinners' College. There were to be no degrees, no credits, no teachers' salaries, but adult education offered to all takers. (No school with such an objective was in existence in New York at the time; the New School for Social Research was opened in 1919.) Cohen was for some years principal or chairman of the executive committee. There were classes in Latin, French, German, algebra, ancient history, modern history, and other high-school level courses, and college-type courses such as courses on the Book of Job, in philosophy, the philosophy of history. The college (also called the Davidson School) also organized clubs, Sunday outings, and a summer camp for weekends and holidays. The attractiveness of the school is indicated by the facts that in 1902-03 there were 783 students in that year in the classes, and that altogether close to 1,400 persons benefited from its program. The Breadwinners' College continued for eighteen years, to 1918 (its program in a way taken up by the New School for Social Research, with which Cohen became identified as the school's first lecturer and where he conducted a weekly course for many years.[19]) Among its lecturers and teachers were, besides Cohen, leading scholars and thinkers including Charles M. Bakewell, W. T. Harris, John Dewey, Edwin R. A. Seligman, and William Allan Neilson. [20]

> It was Thomas Davidson who inspired Cohen to devote days and years to the Breadwinners' College. In May 1900 Davidson wrote to his students in New York: "If you found a Breadwinners' College now, and make it a success, you may live to see a copy of it in every city ward and in every country village....A little knot of earnest Jews has turned the world upside down before now. Why may not the same thing, nay, a far better thing, happen in your day, and among you? Have you forgotten the old promise made to Abraham,--'In thee and in thy seed shall all the families of the earth be blessed'? You can bring the promise to fulfillment if you will. A little heroism, a little self-sacrifice, and the thing is done."[21]

William James had wanted Harvard to appoint Davidson a professor of philosophy—"a kind of Socrates, a devotee of truth and lover of youth, ... a contagious example of how lightly and humanly a burden of learning might be borne...his influence among students would be priceless. ... I think that in this case, Harvard University lost a great opportunity."[22] However, Harvard's loss was Cohen's gain, and a gain for workers and society; for the college, as Cohen wrote, helped "to transform [Jewish] shirt makers into teachers, physicians, biologists, ... engineers... heads of settlements."[23] And it helped to move Morris Cohen into intellectual and spiritual adulthood and into making him the great teacher and great Jew that he was.

III

Cohen received the B. S. degree from City College in 1900. For two years, 1902-04, he was a graduate student in philosophy at Columbia. At the same time he taught mathematics at Townsend Harris Hall, City College's preparatory high school. In 1904 Felix Adler (who had founded the Ethical Culture movement in 1876) arranged for Cohen to go to Harvard on a $750 fellowship. He studied at Harvard for two years and received the Ph.D. degree in 1906. His dissertation was on Kant's theory of happiness. In his second year at Harvard his roommate was Felix Frankfurter, who was graduated from City College in 1902. During that year Cohen was in poor health, and Frankfurter, who was a law student, looked after him. They became lifelong intimate friends. At Harvard Cohen studied under William James and Josiah Royce. He later noted that James was his best friend (a photograph of James was on a wall in the Cohen apartment, and he named his younger son for James), and that Royce was his best teacher, one after whom he wanted to model himself. During his second year, from his close relationship with Frankfurter, Cohen developed an interest in law and legal philosophy that remained with him all his life. Royce frequently mentioned Charles S. Peirce, and Peirce, too, became a lifelong interest of Cohen's, eventually leading to Cohen's pioneering work on behalf of Peirce in editing *Chance, Love, and Logic: Essays of C. S. Peirce* in 1923. While at Harvard, Cohen organized a branch of the Ethical Culture movement.

He left Harvard with letters of recommendation from William James, Royce, George Herbert Palmer, and Ralph Barton Perry. He also had such letters from Felix Adler and William T. Harris. No one could have started out to look for a first position as a teacher of philosophy with better recommendations. Yet he found no open door, nor any welcome. In those early years of the twentieth century, philosophy and religion were closely tied at almost all colleges and universities, and religion meant, of course, Christianity. Cohen went to Townsend Harris Hall to teach mathematics. He was, naturally, unhappy, frustrated, and despondent. Fortunately, in June 1906 he married Mary Ryshpan, who sustained his spirits (as she did until her death in 1942, predeceasing him by five years). At last, in 1912, after a wait of six years, Cohen was appointed assistant professor of philosophy at City College. Before his appointment Cohen published articles and reviews in leading philosophical journals and conducted classes at the Davidson School.

It was as a great teacher at CCNY that Cohen won fame among philosophers and intellectuals. In 1921 he was promoted to full professor. Until his retirement in 1938, after twenty-six years of teaching philosophy, he taught many young men who themselves became professors of philosophy when restrictions on the appointment of Jews became less severe. These former students of Cohen constituted a veritable galaxy of American philosophers; they included Ernest Nagel, Sidney Hook, Lewis S. Feuer, Joseph T. Shipley, Paul Weiss, Joseph Ratner, Daniel J. Bronstein, Philip P. Wiener, Herbert Schneider, Morton White, Milton Munitz, Leo Abraham, and others; Cohen estimated that he had taught at CCNY a total of some fifteen thousand students.

Cohen's method of teaching, in his day, was not of the conventional sort. He was not tied down to a textbook and student recitations, nor did he rely on lectures, but used the Socratic method of questioning the students to elicit a latent idea, directed toward the establishment of a proposition. In his autobiography Cohen explained that he resorted to the Socratic method because when he started to teach philosophy he had found himself devoid of the gift of verbal fluency. As the years passed, perhaps it was in the early 1930s, Cohen felt that his method of teaching had lost some of its sparkle, due to his declining physical energy and to the growing size of his classes, as well as the distraction of outside activities (especially his involvement with Jewish activities); he was questioning less and resorting more to lecturing. He was very critical of his own lecturing, for he feared that "lecturing would unconsciously beget an easy omniscience and satisfaction with apparent or rhetorical truths. No man, no matter how critical, can stand up before a class and refrain from saying more than he knows."[24]

Cohen was well aware that his method of teaching by raising questions and demolishing answers had created the widely held opinion that he was merely negative, destructive. He readily pleaded guilty to the charge. When a student ventured to complain that Cohen was merely critical, he responded: "You have heard the story of how Hercules cleaned the Augean stables. He took the entire dirt and manure out and left them clean. You ask me, 'What did he leave in their stead?' I answer, 'Isn't it enough to have cleaned the stables?'"[25] Cohen wrote that he had learned from Davidson not to succumb to the natural urge to remake God and the universe in one's own image. Davidson, he noted, had made it a rule of his life to quarrel with those who agreed with him, and to have as his favorite students those who most radically differed from him. "Why should I assume," he wrote,

> that my own convictions represented the summit of wisdom in philosophy or anything else? It seemed to me a more important service in the cause of liberal civilization to develop a spirit of genuine regard for the weight of evidence and a power to discriminate between responsible and irresponsible sources of information, to inculcate the habit of admitting ignorance when we do not know, and to nourish the critical spirit of inquiry which is inseparable from the love of truth that makes men free.[26]

Cohen also had acquired a reputation for being acerbic in class as he commented on what students said. At the time of his retirement in 1938 *Time* magazine referred to Cohen as "a modern Socrates with an acid tongue."[27] The testimony of Cohen's former student, Professor Richard B. Morris, of Columbia University, well-known American historian, was, however, that "perhaps two percent of Cohen's students were rankled by his acerbity. For most of us, to be corrected by Socrates seemed neither a surprise nor a disgrace. He cracked down on the fakers. But to the responsive students he was encouraging and generous."[28]

In October 1927, over a thousand persons gathered at the Hotel Astor to honor Professor Cohen to mark his twenty-five years of teaching at City College (including his years at the college's preparatory school). Professor Felix Frankfurter was toastmaster. Among the speakers were Professor Nathan R. Margolis of Harvard Law School, a former student; Dean Frederick J. E, Woodbridge, under whom Cohen had studied philosophy at Columbia; Dr. Judah L. Magnes, president of Hebrew University (which had opened in 1925); Judge Julian W. Mack; Bertrand Russell; Frederick B. Robinson, president of City College; and John Dewey. There were letters from Justice Holmes, Dean Roscoe Pound, Benjamin N. Cardozo (then chief judge of the Court of Appeals of New York), and others.[29] Eight years later, at the age of fifty-seven, Cohen retired, for reasons of health and because he wanted more time for writing, and more time for the Jewish activities that he had started in the early 1930s.

IV

When Cohen was twelve years old, he overheard a conversation between his father and an acquaintance. The latter challenged Abraham Cohen to prove that there is a personal God. To this challenge Mr. Cohen could only reply: "I am a believer." "This," Cohen later wrote, "did not satisfy my own mind. After some reflection I concluded that in all my studies no such evidence was available. After that I saw no reason for prayer or the specifically Jewish religious observances." However, since he lived with his parents in their home, he continued to comply with religious requirements until he was nineteen years old.

Cohen was an agnostic, or what used to be called, especially in England, a rationalist. He would not, however, think of himself as an atheist. "Those who called themselves atheists," he wrote,

> "seemed to be singularly blind, as a rule, to the limitations of our knowledge and to the infinite possibilities beyond us. ... Those of my circle who rejected religion in toto seemed to me to be casting away the ideals that had sustained our people through so many generations. ... In this some of us lost sight of the larger view that Thomas Davidson had taught, that we have no right to break away from the past until we have appropriated all its experience and wisdom, and that reverence for the past may go hand in hand with loyalty to the future, to the Kingdom which doth not yet appear..." [31]

Cohen lived up to the mandate to appropriate from the past all its experience and wisdom. He studied the Bible and other Jewish classics all his life. While a graduate student at Harvard, he studied with Professor George Foot Moore, authority on comparative religion and author of the highly regarded, magisterial three-volume work *Judaism in the First Centuries of the Christian Era* (1927). And Cohen accepted for himself Santayana's definition of piety as "reverence for the sources of one's being."[32] He wrote that it is to be regretted that most Jews had "lost contact with the traditional substance of Jewish education." It is important, he wrote, "for a Jew living in a predominantly non-Jewish world to understand the actual history of his own people. In other words, to lead a dignified, self-respecting life, a Jew must know the history of his people, not merely in the Biblical period, but also in the Talmudic and more recent historic eras."[33] The Hebrew Scriptures, he wrote, "never ceased to grip me," and when he was depressed and had little energy for study or writing, he found the Bible and biblical criticism "most absorbing reading."[34]

Although firmly an agnostic, Cohen wrote that his studies of the great religions had led him to see that ritual is a primary fact in human experience. For himself, he wrote,

> the ancient ceremonies that celebrate the coming and going of life, the wedding ceremony, the *b'rith*, and the funeral service, give an expression to the continuity of the spiritual tradition that is more eloquent than any phrases of my own creation. The ritual may be diluted by English and by modernism, but the Hebraic God is still a potent symbol of the continuous life of which we individuals are waves.

> Like vivid illustrations in the book of my life are the prayers of my parents, ... and the celebration of the continuity of generations in the Passover services in the home of my parents and in the homes of my children. And though I have never gone back to theological supernaturalism, I have come to appreciate more than I once did the symbolism in which is celebrated the human need of trusting to the larger vision, according to which calamities come and go but the continuity of life and faith in its better possibilities survive.[35]

In 1928-29 Cohen undertook the chairmanship of a project called the Talmudic Library. Together with Professor Chaim Tchernowitz (Rav Za'ir), of the Jewish Institute of Religion (later joined to Hebrew Union College), he had a plan to prepare and publish an encyclopedia that would make the Talmud intelligible to general readers, but the time was apparently not ready for this venture. It attracted the support of Professors Moore, John Dewey, Roscoe Pound, and other leading non-Jewish scholars but not enough enthusiasm among Jewish scholars. The idea is currently being implemented by the Israeli *Encyclopedia Talmudica* and by the work of Adin Steinsaltz.

The breadth and depth of Cohen's knowledge of Jewish history and philosophy can easily be seen in his profoundly scholarly essay on "Philosophies of Jewish History,"[36] published in 1939. The essay shows his knowledge of practically all the great masters of Jewish life and thought: Philo, Rashi, Maimonides, Joseph Karo, Graetz, Dubnow, Zinberg, Elijah Gaon of Vilna, Hermann Cohen, Claude Montefiore, Nachman Krochmal, Leoplold Zunz, Abraham Geiger, Zacharias Frankel, Ahad Ha'Am, and many others, not to mention the Bible, the Talmud, and the Apocrypha. It is an essay with encyclopedic sweep and yet it has depth and a personal touch and spirit. Only a master scholar could have written the essay.

As a boy living in Minsk, Cohen became an avid reader of Yiddish novels, and his fondness of Yiddish was sustained throughout his life. He read a Yiddish newspaper. "I owe a good deal of my education," he wrote, "to the Yiddish press. It taught me to look at world news from a cosmopolitan instead of a local or provincial point of view, and it taught me to interpret politics realistically, instead of being misled by empty phrases."[37] The Yiddish press, he noted, prepared millions of Jews to take a worthy part in American civilization and promoted the self-respect to which they were entitled because of their character and history. Furthermore, he gave credit to the Yiddish press, perhaps because it had no army of reporters to dig up sensational news, for emphasizing things of permanent, rather than ephemeral, interest. "It tried to give its readers something of enduring and substantial value."[38]

On the question of Zionism, however, Cohen listened to a different drumbeat. He was not a Zionist. Just as he opposed assimilationism, so, too, he opposed the separatism that Zionism implied. While he greatly admired the *halutzim* who reclaimed the soil of Eretz Israel, and opposed the restrictions on Jewish immigration and land ownership in Palestine imposed by the British government, and supported the establishment and development of the Hebrew University, he felt repulsed by the idea that the establishment of a Jewish state would necessarily mean discrimination against non-Jews. In any case, he felt that Zionism was a distraction of American Jews from the problems they faced at home.

But while Cohen was not a Zionist, he was not an anti-Zionist. Zionism, he wrote in 1945, "has served a high purpose," it has "rendered the supreme service of increasing men's self-respect." Cohen fitted in the Jews and his own awareness of himself as a Jew into his philosophy of pluralism and the desirability of cultural diversity—a philosophy that he shared with Horace M. Kallen. He rejected the notion of nationalism that pervaded Europe, a narrow nationalism that contrasted with American federalism and the idea represented by the motto *E pluribus unum*. Many different peoples have settled America, and each has made its contribution to a common civilization. Why, then, he asked, "should not the Jews contribute their specific gifts? The idea that all immigrants should wipe out their past and become simple imitations of the dominant type is neither possible nor desirable. ...All great civilizations have resulted from the contributions of many peoples, and a richer American culture can come only if the Jews, like other elements, are given a chance to develop under favorable conditions their peculiar genius."[40] In another context he wrote, "Why should not the Jews contribute their specific gifts in the way of enthusiasm for the arts, for social idealism, as well as their peculiar love of intellectual life for its own sake?"[41]

V

In the Spring of 1933, when Cohen was fifty-two years of age, he began to think of retiring from teaching. In 1931, with the help of his son Felix, Cohen's *Reason and Nature* and in 1933 his *Law and the Social Order* had been published, and soon there was to be published *An Introduction to Logic and Scientific Method* (1934) by Cohen and his former student Professor Ernest Nagel. He had been a regular contributor to the *New Republic* from its very conception in 1914; he wrote for it some forty review essays, as well as editorials, some of which were later incorporated into his books.[42] His health was precarious. He could retire with the feeling that, he wrote, what he had to contribute to philosophy would not perish with him. This gave him a sense of relief. But he did not contemplate for his remaining years days of idle reveries. No, he wrote, "with this sense of relief, I could look about me to see what, if anything, the meager offerings of a logician could contribute to the future of my people here and abroad and to the cause of human freedom, with which the fate of the Jew has been so intricately bound for so many centuries."[43]

In 1933 Hitler had come into power. It was no time to merely dabble in Jewish affairs; the dangers loomed large; Cohen decided to devote his major efforts to the problems that the Jewish people faced. From a part-time Jew, Cohen was moving to become a full-time Jew. When he considered his own intellectual equipment and the things that he could best do, Cohen decided that his contribution would best be to research and the application of the scientific method to some basic Jewish interests and needs. Anti-Semitism was rampant and was threatening the very life of the Jewish people. But how much was really known about the causes and nature of anti-Semitism? As he looked about him, Cohen saw the Jewish people hopelessly divided over ideology, religion, Zionism, capitalism and Communism, and other issues. It seemed to him "that the only possible basis of unity was the basis that gives unity to the disagreements of scientists, a common acceptance of the need for demonstrable knowledge, based on nonpartisan scholarly studies." In any case, he wrote, "it seemed worthwhile to try to mobilize intellectual forces for the study of the present and prospective situation of the Jewish people.... Human knowledge and understanding may not enable us to solve all the problems of the Jew in an unjust world, but abandoning the effort to understand the underlying causes and to avoid foreseeable errors is intellectual cowardice."[44] To effectuate this objective, Cohen, with the help of Alvin Johnson, convened a meeting in June 1933 at the New School for Social Research, that was attended by some of Cohen's old associates from the days of Thomas Davidson and others, lawyers, scholars, doctors, economists; and out of this meeting there was organized, a few months later, the Conference on Jewish Relations (which in 1955 became the Conference on Jewish Social Studies).

The Conference was publicly launched in 1936 at a meeting presided over by Albert Einstein and addressed by Cohen, Harold Laski, and Professor Salo W. Baron, who was closely associated with Cohen in this activity. At the conclusion of the meeting, Henry Morgenthau, Sr, made an appeal for funds. The organization was conceived as one that would be directed by scholars for scholarly objectives. It was felt that the research would help in the struggle against Nazi propaganda that was being widely spread throughout the world. But beyond this immediate need, there was also the need for reliable data on Jewish population, the economic composition of the Jewish people, and other relevant aspects of Jewish life.

The Conference launched a number of projects. A major project was the publication of the scholarly quarterly *Jewish Social Studies* in 1939, which marked its fiftieth anniversary in 1989. Cohen was its first editor, as he was also the first president of the Conference. Baron was vice president, as were also Professor Harry A. Wolfson of Harvard, Professor Edward Sapir of Yale, and Dr. Israel Wachsler, famous neurologist. The Conference was not intended to be a propaganda agency or to be anything but a research bureau. Several offshoots of the Conference were the Jewish Occupational Council and the Jewish Cultural Reconstruction, which was in charge of salvaging and redistributing manuscripts, books, artistic, cultural and ritual objects looted by the Nazis from Jewish communities and individuals.

After his retirement from City College in January 1938, Cohen devoted almost all his time and energy to the Conference and its scholarly journal. At the same time many colleges and universities tried to induce him to come as a lecturer or a visiting professor, and he accepted a limited number of the offers, especially from Harvard and the University of Chicago, but always on a restricted schedule that would leave him time for Conference work. His health was poor but he kept pushing himself, and he was always worried and concerned that he was not doing enough in the face of the monumental needs of the Jewish people. With the help of his son Felix, there were published in Cohen's lifetime his *Preface to Logic* (1944), *Faith of a Liberal* (1946), and the book that Cohen thought of as his magnum opus, *The Meaning of Human History* (1947). Nine additional books were published posthumously.

In 1990, more than forty years after his death in 1947, seven of Cohen's books were in print, and the Conference on Jewish Social Studies and the journal *Jewish Social Studies* were still in existence. Morris Raphael Cohen, a man frail in health, a man with a sad face and subject to despondency, a man who came as an immigrant at the age of twelve and who for many years suffered physical and spiritual deprivation, a scholar and teacher whose first book was not published until he was fifty-one years old, yet he was universally recognized as a leading philosopher and thinker. He was elected President of the American Philosophical Association (Eastern Division) in 1929, perhaps the first Jew to have been given this honor.

Cohen's life and work touched the lives of countless people—his former students who themselves became philosophers; jurists, like Justice Holmes and Felix Frankfurter, Jerome Frank and Nathan Margold; Jewish scholars and Jewish communal workers—it has been given to few persons to leave a legacy so rich, so abundant and variant.

Notes

1. See the essay on Kallen by Konvitz in this volume.
2. *A Dreamer's Journey: The Autobiography of Morris Raphael Cohen* (Boston: Beacon Press, 1949) 282. Hereinafter this book will be referred to as *Autob.*
3. Ibid., 283.
4. *Encyclopedia Judaica* 12:967. The Jewish population in 1897 was 4,700, which was 55 percent of the total population.
5. *Autob.,* 32, 33, 35, 39, 40, 57, 165. See also, Leonora Cohen Rosenfield, *Portrait of a Philosopher: Morris R. Cohen in Life and Letters* (New York: Harcourt, Brace & World, 1948), 157. This excellent biography will hereinafter be referred to as *Portrait.*
6. *Autob.* 35.
7. Ibid., 13.
8. Ibid., Foreword.
9. Ibid., 58.
10. Ibid., 91; *Portrait,* 10, 11, 12, 14, 20.
11. *Portrait,* 6.
12. *Autob.* , 93; *Portrait,* 12.
13. *Encyclopedia Judaica,* 12:1093.
14. *Memorials of Thomas Davidson: The Wandering Scholar,* Collected and edited by William Knight (Boston: Ginn and Co., 1907), 13-14. See also *Dictionary of Amer. Biography* (New York: Charles Scribner, 1930-31), Vol. III, Pt. 1, p. 95 (article by Charles M. Bakewell); M, R. Cohen, in *Encyc. of Soc. Sciences,* New York: Macmillan, 1931) 5:10. See also, Thomas Davidson, *The Education of the Wage Earners* (Boston: Ginn and Co., 1904), edited with an introduction by Chas. M. Bakewell. For a bibliography of Davidson's publications, see *Memorials of Thomas Davidson,* 235-238.
15. *Autob.* 121-122.
16. Ibid., 108, 281.
17. *Portrait,* 54.
18. Ibid., 52.
19. Ibid., 144.
20. Ibid., 55. For William James's tribute to Davidson, see *Memorials of Thomas Davidson,* 107, and James, *Memories and Studies* (New York: Longmans, Green, 1924), 73.
21. *Portrait,* 60.
22. William James in *Memorials of Thomas Davidson,* 111-112.
23. *Portrait,* 62.
24. *Autob.* , 158.
25. Ibid., 146.
26. Ibid., 146.
27. *Portrait,* 157.
28. Ibid., 96.
29. *A Tribute to Professor Morris Raphael Cohen, Teacher and Philosopher* (New York: Published by the Youth Who Sat At His Feet, 1928).
30. *Autob.,* 69-70.
31. Ibid., 215.
32. Ibid., 229.
33. Ibid., 230

34. Ibid., 231.
35. Ibid., 218.
36. The essay was published in the first issue of *Jewish Social Studies*, 1: 39 (1939). It is reprinted in one of Cohen's posthumously published books, *Reflections of a Wondering Jew* (Boston: Beacon Press, 1950), 53.
37. *Autob.,* 219.
38. Ibid., 220.
39. Ibid., 226,
40. Ibid., 220.
41. *Reflections of a Wondering Jew*, 33.
42. *Portrait*, 429.
43. *Autob.* , 236.
44. Ibid., 240-241.

3

Sidney Hook

Sidney Hook (1902-1989) was a leading American social philosopher. He taught philosophy at New York University from 1927 to 1972. He was the author of at least a score of books. Originally a Marxist, he became a leading anticommunist thinker and was active in anticommunist causes. In his philosophy he was closely identified with the thought of John Dewey. His chief interests were social and political thought, and the defense of political democracy and socialist democracy (or democratic socialism). Soon after he received the Presidential Medal of Freedom from President Ronald Reagan in 1985, he said, "I am an unreconstructed believer in the welfare state and in a steeply progressive income tax, a secular humanist, and a firm supporter of freedom of choice with respect to abortion, voluntary euthanasia, and other domestic measures to which he [President Reagan] is opposed." His individualism and belief in freedom were coupled with a deep sense of moral and social responsibility. He identified himself with cultural pluralism, political democracy, economic welfare, and the central importance of intelligence in the life of man and society. Although an agnostic, or perhaps an atheist, he made common cause with all who struggled for religious freedom. He was not involved in organized Jewish political or religious life, he identified himself with the Jewish Labor Committee, and maintained that Jews had a legitimate desire to survive as a group, whether the group is defined by religion, culture, or historical continuity. See Paul Kurtz, ed., *Sidney Hook and the Contemporary World* (1968).

* * *

I

Reflecting upon his own intellectual life, soon after he had passed his seventieth birthday, Sidney Hook wrote,

> I have, to be sure, learned a great deal about man and society during the half century almost that has elapsed since reaching philosophical self-consciousness. It has led me time and again to rethink my basic commitment to the pragmatic philosophy and hopefully to a more nuanced and subtle expression of my views. Nonetheless I have found no adequate ground for abandoning or radically modifying my basic position.

Then quickly followed an afterthought. Turning away from looking into his own intellectual history, and looking out on the state of the world about him, he added, with an obvious sadness of conviction, that he and his philosophical colleagues had "assumed too easily that the achievement of intellectual conviction carried with it the moral courage to act on it. Unfortunately, this has not been the case, especially in recent years."

We, however, surveying the same scene, and having before us the record of Sidney Hook's half-century of thought and action, can readily affirm that Hook has himself been an exception to the fact that he so correctly observed. In a singular and towering way, he has had the moral courage to act on his intellectual convictions. His mind, no less than his heart, has always been touched with fire. Thought and action have always been linked, not only in his pragmatic philosophy, but also in his life from day to day. As I look upon that life that Sidney Hook has lived, I cannot help but hear in my mind the words spoken by Justice Holmes in a Memorial Day address a century ago: "I think that, as life is action and passion [only Hook would say "thought" rather than "passion"], it is required of a man that he should share the passion and action of his time at peril of being judged not to have lived." No one will ever be able to say that Sidney Hook had not lived. The reasonable man, he has written, "has impulses but is not impulsive, has emotions but is not emotional, and understands what William James meant about the importance of moral holidays." But Hook himself had not taken moral holidays, or intellectual holidays, or any other holidays. Perhaps even outdoing the watcher of Israel, Sidney Hook neither slumbered nor slept. Many of us would ourselves have been more wakeful and more watchful had there been no Sidney

Hook out there proving to us that "the achievement of intellectual conviction carried with it the moral courage to act on it." There has been great reliance on him as a surrogate who would effectively expose abuses and usurpations, injuries and oppressions, and the widespread trust in the messenger and his message has never been misplaced. He seems to be blessed with endless vitality; his writings never revealed a weariness of thought, a slackening of intellectual energy or moral concern. One is tempted to apply to Hook the words of Jeremiah, "great in counsel and mighty in work, whose eyes are open upon all the ways of the sons of men." Readers of his many books and countless articles know that, in one way or another, Sidney Hook had the compulsion and the genius always to point to the higher values, to touch the mainsprings of one's better self, to propel one towards a fuller life and the more enduring joys of life.

More than any other contemporary American, Sidney Hook can be classified among the *philosophes,* thinkers who not only study the world, but who also try to change it; thinkers who act upon the moral, intellectual, and spiritual world that is the subject of their study; thinkers whose concern with the eternal or ultimate questions does not keep them from a concern with the immediate and intermediate questions that they, together with the rest of mankind, face. Hook reminds us that it is not necessary for people to agree about the meaning of ethical terms before they can determine the best moral policy "with respect to, for example, health care, the reduction of poverty, or treatment of crime." Our value problems, he says, are specific, and "if we take them one at a time, we do not have to settle questions about so-called ultimate values or goals. Our problem is always what to do in this particular case; if I discover that this action rather than another will win friendship (or health or knowledge or money), I do not have to inquire what these are good for or whether they are worth having." But of course, like Plato or Aristotle, like Kant or Hegel, Hook knew how and when to raise questions about ultimate values or goals; but what marked him off from the conventional professional philosophers is that he was equally at home in the realm of practicalities as in the realm of abstractions. "I do not," he said, "have to be in possession of an ultimate or absolute value in order to choose what is desirable among possible alternatives." Many solutions are quite acceptable even though they fall short of being ideal.

Thus, while freely at home in the community of fellow philoso-phers—Hook was president of the American Philosophical Associa-tion (Eastern Division) 1959-60,—he was unique among them in en-joying a worldwide audience for his articles in the *New York Times Magazine, Commentary, Encounter, American Scholar, Humanist,* and other journals of public opinion and public affairs, and as a founder and leader of the Conference on Methods in Philosophy and Science, the American Committee for Cultural Freedom, the Conference on Scientific Spirit and Democratic Faith, the University Centers for Ra-tional Alternatives, and the League for Industrial Democracy. When intellectuals in Europe, in Latin America, in Japan or Israel would try to think of a colleague in contemporary America, in most cases the first name that would come to them was that of Sidney Hook.

A poignant example of how ultimate and immediate problems and values are interlocked in the mind of Hook is the statement he wrote for his biography in *Who's Who in America* as a reflection upon his principles and ideals:

> It is better to be a live jackal than a dead lion - for jackals, not men. Those who have the moral courage to fight intelligently for freedom have the best pros-pects of avoiding the fate of both live jackals and dead lions. Survival is not the be-all and end-all of a life worthy of man. Sometimes the worst thing we can know about a man is that he has survived. Those who say life is worth living at any cost have already written for themselves an epitaph of infamy, for there is no cause and no person they will not betray to stay alive. Man's vocation should be the use of the arts of intelligence in behalf of human freedom.

II

Born in New York in 1902 and brought up in working-class areas of the city, Hook at an early age discovered in himself a strong social interest that almost naturally propelled him toward the writings of Marx and Engels. But also in his youth he was fascinated by philo-sophical inquiry, he recalls how his imagination was fired by the amateur epistemological discussion in Jack London's *Martin Eden.* Early in his life, too, he was exposed to books by Henry Charles Lea, William Edward Lecky, and John W. Draper, and thus found himself in a rationalistic revolt against superstition and organized religion, a position that was strengthened as he experienced or observed religious intolerance and discrimination.

At the College of the City of New York, Hook studied under Morris Raphael Cohen, whom he later described as the first critical mind he had encountered in the educational wilderness, and who gave him a sense for logical method and evidence. The study of logic led Hook to metaphysics and to the works of Bertrand Russell. As a graduate student at Columbia, he first came under the influence of Frederick J. E. Woodbridge, from whose "modified Aristotelianism" he was led away by John Dewey. It was Dewey who had the most enduring intellectual and personal influence on Hook.

One must exercise caution, however, in speaking of intellectual influences on a person who by temperament is unable to be a follower. Hook could be a friend but not a disciple. He selected from Marx and Engels, from Cohen and Russell, from Woodbridge and Dewey only those elements in their thoughts and ways of thinking that appealed to him and could meet the tests imposed by his own critical faculty. His own temperament played crucial selective and directive roles in the way his thoughts developed and the lines of action he chose to take from time to time. Hook himself wrote that there is a connection between temperament and thought. The former, he wrote,

> which loves peace above all other values and sees in the ordered routines of professional, social, and personal life the best methods of achieving it is likely to embrace in thought the calm options of eternity and invariance, if not the consolations of outright theology. The temperament which enjoys battle, for which variety is a genuine good, which values the perplexities that attend the pursuit of incompatible goods as the opportunities for creative action, is likely to follow the vital option of experimentalism.

He has also noted that, at least in extreme situations, reason alone does not determine the course of action. Character and habit, among other things, also play a role. No one, of course, Hook has noted, has a temperament that loves only peace or only battle, but the dominant pattern will assert itself. There can be little doubt that by temperament Hook loves battle, variety, coping with the perplexities that attend the confrontation between competing values, and that the path he generally follows is that of experimentalism.

III

Hook has variously described or named his *Weltanschauung* as experimentalism, or experimental naturalism, or pragmatic naturalism. More recently, however, he called it simply pragmatism, or as "the philosophy of pragmatism in the tradition of Charles S. Peirce and John Dewey." His basic conviction is that "there is only one reliable method of reaching the truth about the nature of things anywhere and at any time," and that "this reliable method comes to full fruition in the methods of science." Most recently Hook has written that in its broadest sense as a philosophy of life, pragmatism "holds that the logic and ethics of scientific method can and should be applied to human affairs." This implies, he went on to say, "that one can make warranted assertions about values as well as facts." Although Hook's pragmatism recognizes that there are differences between questions of fact and questions of value, and that the latter require the use of different methods of inquiry and testing in ascertaining objective knowledge about them, nonetheless pragmatism "holds that it is possible to gain objective knowledge not only about the best means available to achieve given ends, something freely granted, but also about the best ends in the problematic situations in which the ends are disputed or become objects of conflict."

Despite, however, his repeated stress on scientific method and his claims for its far-reaching relevance and applicability, Hook generally succeeds in avoiding the charge of scientism, which critics are prone to make, by recognizing the legitimacy of "reason," "intelligence," or "common sense." Even though the scientific method is of supreme importance, it is not an "absolute." There is a legitimate place for even "good sense," which, "like a sense of tact or humor," has "as deep a root in our generic structure as in our learned behavior." What it all comes down to are that there may be so many relevant factors entering a decision, "regardless of whether the issue is political, personal or scientific,"

> that one cannot formulate a rule prescribing reasonable behavior in all conceivable circumstances. What seems warranted is the assertion that given the concrete circumstances of any decision, investigation will show that all possible decisions are not equally justifiable, that some are better than others...

The important point to be noted here is that Hook's pragmatism includes more, far more, than dedication to scientific method. It includes the use of and reliance on intelligence, reason, common sense, good sense, and, as evidenced by his *Who's Who* statement of belief, as well as by other statements to which we will soon refer, a strong commitment to certain ideals of life which a decent person will hold even in the face of death. Hook's pragmatism effectively limits his naturalism and scientific temper. Hook emphasizes that man lives in an open universe in which our own ideas and actions play a creative role. What we choose to do makes a difference. We can influence events. There is no foreordination that should make us optimists or pessimists. With William James, Hook believes that a meliorist attitude towards life and the world is justified. Man is not powerless as he faces the world, for the outer world is not closed but an open world, an unfinished world, one that man can, by his own actions, make better or worse. Pragmatism, as formulated by Hook,

> denies nothing about the world or man which one truly finds in them, but it sees in men something which is at once ... more wonderful and more terrible than anything else in the universe, the power to make themselves and the world around them better or worse.

Against every cult of inevitability, whether it be a form of religious Providence or predestination, or a form of Marxist historical materialism, or Bertrand Russell's "free man's" or Stoic quietism, Sidney Hook consistently and insistently teaches the moral necessity to think for oneself, to act knowingly, to give to challenges that we face a total intellectual, moral, and spiritual response.

For ideas are not mere consolations. They are that, but ideas are also tools that must be used, that can be vindicated, that must be tested. The scientific method is generally the best way we have to subject ideas to the test of experience. And to do this, Hook maintains, is a *moral duty*. The scientific testing of ideas is morally responsible action. It is hard to tell from his writing whether Hook intends to place his main emphasis on the moral necessity to use the scientific method or on his belief in man's freedom to make the world better or worse. The two ideas are, of course, interdependent, and this, I think, is where Hook would choose to place the emphasis. It is a moral imperative to extend the use of the scientific method to man and society, because it is through the application of the scientific method that the frontiers of knowledge and truth are extended, and because it is through the application of the scientific method that man can best assert his freedom to bring about a better, richer, more wholesome and fuller life for himself and humanity, and thus man may succeed to extend the frontiers of his freedom: freedom from ignorance, freedom from what Bertrand Russell spoke of as Fate.

It would be wrong, however, to suggest that Hook believes that man's freedom is an absolute one. We are only relatively free. Our options are not limitless. We act within limits. But within these limits, we are free to act. Were our options limitless, the world would be an anarchic place. He would need an infinite time to choose among infinite possibilities—under such circumstances, the will would in effect be paralyzed, and there would be no room for action at all.

IV

Man's relative freedom does not move in a vacuum. There are values that beckon for recognition and selection. And finally, one does not "have to be in possession of an ultimate or absolute value in order to choose what is desirable among possible alternatives. ... We have *many* 'ultimate' values: love, work, knowledge, family, and friendship, art, country. Our problems result because they conflict with each other." Some values are compatible; some are incompatible, with each other. Some differences can be resolved by reason, some only by conflict. What is demanded is reasonableness; however, reasonableness "is not synonymous with sweet compliance nor does it exclude the judicious use of force. What it requires only is the offer ... to negotiate conflict in the hope of reaching an acceptable, even if not ideal, solution." The process of reasoning cannot be expected to go on indefinitely. A reasonable man must know when it is time to stop reasoning; and reason "is the judge of its own legitimate use and limitation. Reason is not so much *reasoning* as it is good sense."

Values or principles "are a necessary but not a sufficient guide, for the simple reason that more than one principle is involved." And the number of factors that almost invariably enter into a decision are so many, whether the issue is political, personal, or scientific, "that one cannot formulate a rule prescribing reasonable behavior in all conceivable circumstances." There is no Golden Rule, Hook would say, unless it is the commandment or necessity to be reasonable: "What seems warranted is the assertion that given the concrete circumstances of any decision, investigation will show that all possible decisions are not equally justifiable, that some are better than others..."

In the most important decisions we are called upon to make, as well as in the ordinary affairs of each day, reason never operates alone but always in relation to our fears and hopes, desires and passions. But reason is not their slave because its insight and foresight give us some power to reconstruct them [i. e., our fears and hopes, desires and passions] and to modify the attitudes we bring to the assessment of fact. There is a continuum of ends and means in our attempt to think our way out of our predicaments. The means we select to realize our ends predetermine the ends, which in turn lead, us to modify the means. ... Means are not merely means but integral parts of the end.

Reason, then, always faces alternatives, among which it must make a choice, a decision. There are many "ultimate" values; none among them is absolute; each makes its own bid for recognition and choice. The fanatic is one who knows what his goal or end is and is willing to sacrifice everything else to it, "to repudiate all the other ends of life for the sake of one overriding concern or supreme end. No matter how exalted the supreme end may be, whether knowledge or art, love or friendship, pleasure or purity, justice or glory, whoever is prepared to sacrifice all other ends to it is a moral monster."

It is not clear, however, how this last statement is consistent with Hook's formulation in *Who's Who*, which asserts that in an extreme situation a decent person should choose to die rather than betray a cause. To me this means that a moral person may feel compelled, in an extreme case, to act as a "fanatic," and that Hook would approve, and even commend, such an action. Thomas More chose to become a dead lion rather than to continue to live but as a live jackal. As he walked to his death, Thomas More was no fanatic in a pejorative sense. In his own honorable way, he made his substantial contribution to human freedom. There are, then, situations in which a person must be prepared to sacrifice all other ends to a supreme end that is so exalted that he is willing and ready to give up even his life for it.

In a war, is not every fighting soldier in such a situation? Whether or not he has reasoned his way into his condition, he is in it none the less. In a non-pejorative sense, every soldier, ready to sacrifice his life for his country, is a fanatic, and somehow relates himself with Thomas More, Giordano Bruno, Socrates, and countless other, named and nameless, martyrs, who, not without reason, chose to become dead lions rather than be guilty of an unthinkable betrayal. There are, indeed, times when a man must feel compelled to say, with Luther, *Ich kann nicht anders*. At such a time he acts *as if* there is a supreme end, an absolute, a Golden Rule, an ultimate ideal, a commandment which he *must* obey, no matter at what cost. He has reached a point at which reasoning has terminated, even if it means that his life, too, must then terminate.

This does not necessarily mean that there are values which all men will agree are ultimate or absolute; but perhaps all will agree that every person ought to believe that there are, indeed, some values or ideals which he may one day feel compelled to vindicate at the cost of his life *as if* they ought to be universally considered ultimate or absolute. "Few human beings will contest the statements," says Hook, "that sight is better than blindness, knowledge better than ignorance, health than illness, and freedom than slavery, and that as a rule truthfulness, gratitude, fidelity, sincerity, friendship, kindness, and so on, are preferable to their opposites." "With rare exceptions," Hook has written, "human beings are not so simply organized that they can live at peace with themselves if, for the sake of survival, they betray friends, family, country, and the very ideals and values that are integral to their personalities." We have," Hook has said, "*many* 'ultimate' values: love, work, knowledge, family, friendship, art, and country." It is true, of course, that "problems result because they conflict with each other." But when the conflict is resolved, when one value comes out as the victor, then is it not, then and there, *ultimate* without quotation marks?

This point should not be taken in any way that would minimize the fact, insistently made by Hook, that our moral predicament arises because our values are competitive. Our inner struggles are seldom between good and evil; more often they are between one good and another: between work and play, between truthfulness and kindness, between prudence and generosity. We pray, "Lead us not into temptation." But the temptation is often not an evil but a lesser good, the instant gratification of a lesser good in place of a deferred gratification of a more enduring good. Our agony of choice, Hook has observed, "results from the realization that right conflicts with right, good with good, and sometimes the right with the good. We want both security and adventure and can't have both. We want to be just but discover we cannot be just without being cruel. We want to be loyal, but if we are, we can't be truthful, and vice versa. We want to be free to live our life but find that we cannot do so except on the ruins of another's life. These are typical moral dilemmas. To the extent that we resolve moral conflicts, one right or good is sacrificed to another." Sidney Hook is altogether right in placing stress on this point, which is at the heart of the human predicament and so often the cause of heartbreak.

But when Hook goes beyond this and asserts categorically that "there is no one *alleinseligmachende Wert*, no specific all-sanctifying value, that one upholds at all costs in all circumstances," one feels compelled to recall his poignant, and commendable statement in his *Who's Who* biography as a testament that reflects the principle in Judaism that there are circumstances in which it is commanded by *halacha*, by law, that a person must choose to die rather than perform the act that he is commanded to do: If he is commanded, under threat of death, to perform an act of idolatry, or to kill another person, or to engage in an act of immorality (such as incest or adultery), he must refuse to do the act and must, instead, choose to die—choose to be a dead lion rather than a live jackal.

V

Sidney Hook raises the question, "is it at all plausible to hold that although ethically there can be no absolute human rights, there can or should be absolute constitutional rights, political or juridical freedoms, which may never be abridged in any circumstances?" Hook addressed this question repeatedly over the years, in many of his writings, and one of his most important contributions to constitutional thought has been his concern with and resolution of this deeply significant problem.

Those who regard themselves as absolutists have, says Hook, overlooked a number of important considerations: (1) The concept of freedom cannot be totally open-ended. Obviously we must limit the freedom of criminals and madmen (the jury verdict and the court's judgment in the case of John W. Hinckley, Jr., who attempted to assassinate President Reagan, dramatically focused attention on this aspect of the problem of freedom). Not all freedoms can be enjoyed or are desirable. "The cry for freedom is always a demand for a specific freedom, for something that can be defended as reasonable, for a justified claim. It is inescapably normative." (2) A demand for a specific freedom entails a restriction on another person's freedom. If I am to have freedom of speech, then others are not free to demand that I be prevented from speaking. If the union is free to strike, then others are not free to enjoin or punish the strikers. (3) Our freedoms are often incompatible. Freedom of speech may affect a man's right to a fair trial. Freedom of knowledge may be an invasion of another's right of privacy.

On the central problem of freedom of speech and communication, Hook takes his stand with the position of Justices Holmes and Brandeis, one that he characterizes as "realistic liberalism." In brief, the position is that freedom of speech in a democratic society is of strategic importance. But though this freedom has central importance, we must recognize

> that at certain times, places, and occasions, in the interest of preserving the whole cluster of freedoms essential to a functioning democracy, some expressions may have to be curbed. I do not believe that one criterion or test can be found that will satisfy our reflective moral sense in all situations where some limit on expression is justified.

There are times and occasions when "reasonable and temporary" limitation on speech is necessary and justified, in behalf of other human rights. If talk may not literally kill, "it can trigger the action that does kill." Sometimes, "in the interest of preserving the entire structure of our desirable freedoms, we may be compelled to abridge one or another of our strategic freedoms for a limited time or in a limited place."

Since the problem that we face is one presented by the competition of different freedoms, Justice Frankfurter's notion of "balancing" is relevant and useful. Professor Hook, after a careful analysis of the arguments against "balancing" that have been offered by Justice Black and others, concludes that in the end they turn out to be

> variations of the view that it is dangerous and ultimately disastrous to make exceptions to general rules. Many effective replies can be made to these arguments, but it is enough to say that, granting the danger of making exceptions to general rules, it is sometimes more dangerous and harmful not to make exceptions.

In another context, Hook has said, "If the talk is likely to precipitate violence in consequence of the speaker's incitement, he should be barred. The line may be hard to draw but it is the precise task of intelligence to draw it. ... *Sometimes* it is necessary to pass a red light to avoid a disastrous accident, and to fight fire with fire."

In another essay, he asks, "after all, what is our intelligence for, if not to find appropriate stopping places?" Perhaps more than any other philosopher or critic in our time, Hook exposed the flimsiness and foolishness of the slippery-pole argument: If you give an inch, how do you know where to stop? If one were to take the slippery-pole argument seriously, one would never shake hands, or hold hands, or start eating or drinking, or start a lecture. One recalls the statement of Justice Holmes, which reaches out far beyond the limits of the case before him: "The power to tax is not the power to destroy while this court sits." This is not to say that it is always easy to know where to draw the line. Every legislator, every judge, every parent, every neighbor, every friend, every person, if he is not criminally corrupt or insane, continually faces this problem, and continually resolves the problem. It is a lifelong process, which ends only with the end of life itself.

It should be noted, however, that Justice Frankfurter's "balancing" process no longer plays a significant role in the Supreme Court's jurisprudence, at least not on the expressed or ostensible level of adjudication. The "compelling interest" and "strict scrutiny" approach have largely displaced it. When a right or an interest is involved, such as the Court has found to be a "fundamental" right, a term that encompasses more than what Hook means by "strategic" right, or when the legislation or action attacked is such as to adversely affect a "discrete and insular" minority, constituting a "suspect" classification, then the action or legislation under attack is subject to "strict scrutiny" by the Court. For example, in *Shapiro v. Thompson* (1969), the Supreme Court had before it statutes under which welfare assistance was denied to persons who had not resided within their jurisdictions for at least one year.

The Court, using the compelling interest test, held these acts unconstitutional as an impingement upon the affected persons' fundamental right to travel freely from state to state. These statutes were "suspect" for the reason that the classification "touched on the fundamental right of interstate movement." The Court said, "Since the classification here touches on the fundamental right of interstate movement, its constitutionality must be judged by the stricter standard of whether it promotes a *compelling* state interest."

The new test of constitutionality, which has been used by the Court since the 1960s, does not change the fact that what the Court is called upon to do is to make a choice between two competing rights or interests. On the one hand, there was the reasonable fear of states that the elimination of a reasonable residence requirement would result in a heavy influx of individuals into the states providing the most generous welfare benefits. On the other hand there was the contention that all citizens are constitutionally free to travel throughout the length and breadth of the land uninhibited by laws which impose burdens on needy persons. The argument of the states that the waiting period of one year facilitates the planning of the welfare budget was not such a "compelling governmental interest" as to override the exercise of the needy person's fundamental right to travel. In a sense, one may argue, the Court was still engaged in a "balancing" process, but the process is one that is much more weighted in favor of fundamental rights as against a conventional governmental right. The new process involves the principle that some rights, denominated as "fundamental," are of a higher dignity than other rights; that legislation curtailing such fundamental rights must be subjected, in judicial review, to a scrutiny that is "strict"; that such legislation will not pass such an examination in the absence of the state establishing, to the Court's satisfaction, that the statute reasonably advances the state's "compelling interest" and that it is narrowly tailored to serve that interest. I think that it can be safely said that Justice Frankfurter, who died in 1965, would not have accepted the new constitutional development, for he strongly believed that the Court must exercise stern self-restraint in interfering with the popular will as expressed in legislation enacted by the people's representatives. He thought that in this respect he was following in the footsteps of Justice Holmes, the Court's most vigorous proponent of the philosophy of "judicial restraint." He did not agree that some constitutional rights or liberties enjoyed a "preferred" place, or that some issues justified "strict scrutiny." Frankfurter considered that the "enduring contribution of Mr. Justice Holmes to American history is his constitutional philosophy." This judgment is still valid, but it is doubtful that one could make the same belated judgment about Justice Frankfurter's own contribution.

While all this, I submit, needs to be said, it does not lessen Sidney Hook's contribution to American constitutional philosophy. His emphasis on the point that while some rights may be of "strategic" importance, none can be considered as an absolute, and his argument that rights do not appear in isolation but in contest one with the other, are lessons which constantly need to be freshly learned. How these lessons are to be applied in constitutional adjudication depends on many factors. As case follows case, and as one member of the Court succeeds another, and as the dominant forces of our society shift and change, and as new values emerge, the public law undergoes development, introducing higher levels of sophistication and complexity. For Holmes, as Frankfurter said, "The Constitution was not primarily a text for dialectic but a means of ordering the life of a progressive people." The ordering of that life calls for new insights no less than for past reason, the recognition of new needs as well as enduring ideals.

"To be sure," Hook has written,

> the weight of experience is behind the moral injunctions and ideals expressed in the testaments and commandments of the great religious and ethical systems of the past. But they cannot all be categorical in all situations because they obviously conflict.... The only absolute is, in John Erskine's phrase, echoing a thought of John Dewey, "the moral obligation to be intelligent" in the choice of that course of conduct among possible alternatives whose consequences will strengthen the structure of the reflective values that define our philosophy of life.

The logic of Sidney Hook's thought on freedom, I think, brings him close to the new position of the Supreme Court, which has replaced the "balancing" test of Frankfurter. "By freedom," he has written, "I do not mean the right to do anything one pleases ... but the strategic freedoms of speech, press, assembly, independent trade unions and an independent judiciary, and the cluster of rights associated with democracy in its widest sense. Although they are interrelated, there is an order of priority in freedoms to guide us when they conflict." That order of priorities, I assume, car be determined only by the reflective, critical intelligence, case by case, from time to time. No voice out of Sinai will be heard to resolve such conflicts, but only the still small voice of reason.

VI

As Hook applied his pragmatic philosophy to social organization, he saw himself as a socialist or as a social democrat. He did not hold to the theory of historical materialism; he was no economic determinist. In our own era, since at least World War I, Hook said, "the mode of political decision seems to me to have had at least as much influence on our culture as the mode of economic production." This, "he added, "is not a matter that can be established by conceptual analysis but by empirical, social, and historical inquiry."

Hook was not afraid that governmental intervention in economic affairs must necessarily lead to totalitarianism. There are today socialized economies in totalitarian, despotic countries, but Hook maintained that in all these cases political democracy was destroyed *before* the economy was socialized. Moreover, he noted, "There is not a single democratic country where the public sector of the economy has grown substantially over the years, whether through socialization or through governmental controls and subsidies (whether it be England, Sweden, Norway, Holland, or the United States), in which the dire predictions concerning the extinction or even the radical restrictions of democratic freedoms have been realized." The control or regulation of the economy in the United States has not led to a diminution of the political or cultural freedoms. Although there can be a terrorist regime in the absence of Communism, the absolute control of the economy by a Communist party enables it "to reinforce a kind of terror beyond anything previously known in human history, and to use the bread-card and the work-card to enforce conformity."

From history and the world as we know it today, Hook concluded that the collectivization of major industries has in it the potential to transform the economy into a powerful engine of human repression with the consequential loss of political freedom. "Therefore," Hook said, "in the interests of freedom, it is wiser and safer to limit carefully the extent of socialization." In the interests of human rights and freedoms, it is important to preserve a private sector, to encourage considerable private enterprise, to have some regulated industries and some public corporations, to encourage cooperatives, increased worker participation in the operation of industrial plants as well as in the boards of directors of large corporations, and to develop other means of multiplying centers of economic power.

Hook's socialism is, quite obviously, an economic system that operates within a democratic order. It is democratic socialism, hardly or but barely an *ism*. It is free from dogmatism. It contemplates a mixed economy, in which the mixing is determined by considerations of welfare and freedom. "The emphasis," said Hook, "must be placed not so much on the *legal form* of property relations but on the moral ideals of democracy as a way of life, conceived as an equality of concern for all citizens of the community to develop themselves as persons to their full growth. The economy should be considered a means to that end."

Again we see that to Hook, moral and political concerns are primary. He did not endorse a free enterprise uncontrolled economy. Neither Adam Smith nor Karl Marx is his prophet. What will best serve the nation is an economic order that will preserve our basic democratic values and yet maximize the individual's opportunities for self-development, an order that allows "the judicious development of the democratic welfare state pruned of its bureaucratic excrescence." "Morality," Hook has written, "must have primacy over all social phenomena..."

<h2 style="text-align:center">VII</h2>

As we have seen, Sidney Hook did not hesitate to redefine and reinterpret such terms as pragmatism and socialism. The use and abuse of such and other terms by obscurantists and fanatics did not drive him to invent his own vocabulary, a device often resorted to by philosophers, only to add new obscurities and compound the difficulties of understanding. Yet Hook would not reinterpret "God," and in the list of strategic freedoms, which we quoted above, there is a noticeable absence of "religion." In this matter, Hook chose a path other than that taken by William James and John Dewey. Perhaps in this he is wiser than most of us? "God," said St. Augustine, "is best known in not knowing Him." And Maimonides said essentially the same. There is a respectable tradition for God as *deus absconditus.* I would not venture to speak for God, but it is hard to repress the thought that God wishes that the world had more persons who are uncertain of Him in the way of Sidney Hook, and less of those who claim to know Him by name, address, occupation, relatives, friends, enemies. There are gentle religions that teach that God finds most acceptable not those who call on Him by name but those who follow the paths of peace, freedom, and righteousness. God may well be the greatest pragmatist of all, judging ideas and men not by their presuppositions but by their consequences, by their fruit. "We say," Emerson wrote, "that every man is entitled to be valued by his best moment. We measure our friends so." It is thus that we measure Sidney Hook. Would God do less?

Although in his *Weltanschauung* Hook found no place or function for God, he was quite comfortable with his Jewish roots and with being a Jew. When, about nine months before his death in July 1989, he was interviewed by Norman Podhoretz, the then editor of *Commentary,* he said that a Jewish atheist is not a contradiction, the combination of the two words is not an oxymoron, for the Jewish atheist is still a Jew. If he could be reborn after death, would he choose to do so? Yes, he said, he would choose to be reborn, and as a Jew.

Hook regretted that he had a poor Jewish education in a traditional *heder,* and he regretted, too, that he did not provide a proper Jewish education for his children, and that his grandchildren lack a Jewish consciousness. A reason for Jewish education, he said, "is to be able to accept yourself as a Jew and to try to build a life of dignity on that basis. That's a great difficulty many people have with my position. I am not a religious Jew, I am not a political Zionist, and though I have been a strong believer in supporting Israel ever since it was established by the United Nations—they have the same right to their existence as any other people. I'm not a scholar in Hebrew or in Aramaic. And yet I'm a Jew and I feel that I'm a Jew." He recalled that he attended the organizational meeting of the Conference on Jewish Relations, convened by Morris Raphael Cohen and Salo W. Baron, and that he felt embarrassed: "I said to myself then, all those meetings I have gone to so far for radical causes and sectarian causes, why not for Jewish causes? It was a turning point in my awareness." He then began to work against anti-Semitism, "and I worked with the *Jewish Frontier* [the Labor Zionist journal] and the Reconstructionists."

It is clear from the record that at the center of his life was the central Jewish belief that people have the power, and the duty, "to make themselves and the world around them better," that *tikkun ha-olam*, the improvement of the world, the enhancement of life, is the chief reason and value of man's life. By his life Sidney Hook bore witness to the truth and significance of the saying of Maimonides that "God gave man the power to reason, which makes man capable of perfection," only Hook would add, "and capable of perfecting the world."

Four years before his death, Professor Hook put to me in a letter the following question: "whether there is anything in traditional Jewish theology which explicitly declares that the morally right or wrong, good or bad can be determined without reference to God. ...Is there anything in the writings of Maimonides or other Jewish theologians, or in the writings of the prophets, rabbis or holy men that suggest good or bad, right or wrong can be determined independently of any presupposition of God's existence?"

Over a span of many years Hook put to me, by letter or, more often, by long-distance telephone call, questions about Judaism. In Jerusalem there is a congregation made up of Jewish men and women who identify themselves as Jews who "seek the way," *mevakshe derech*. If Hook had lived in Jerusalem in one of his sabbatical years, he might have found the spirit of such a congregation congenial; he would have appreciated the proposition that study is a form of worship, a form of piety. It all depends on the spirit.

Rabbi Moshe Leib of Sasov taught that there is no quality and no power of man that serves no purpose. What purpose, he was asked, does the denial of God serve? "Ah!" he said, the atheist serves a great purpose. "For if someone comes to you and asks your help, you shall not turn him off with pious words, saying, 'Have faith and take your troubles to God!' You shall act as if there were no God..." According to the ancient rabbis, "God says, 'Would that they, had deserted Me, but kept My Law!'"

"In France," said Charles Augustin Sainte-Beuve; "we remain Catholics after we have ceased to be Christians." I think that it may be said of Sidney Hook, as also of Horace M. Kallen and of Morris Raphael Cohen, that he remained a Jew after he ceased to be a Judaist. Such Jews, in their own special way, lift up the world.

In his preface to the Hebrew translation of his *Totem and Taboo*, Freud wrote that although he had given up a great deal that he might have had in common with other Jews, yet what remained of his Jewishness was "still a great deal, probably the main thing." As Peter Gay observed, the essence of Freud's Jewishness escaped and resisted his understanding, he remained the "Godless Jew," the "infidel Jew." All this, I submit, can with equal conviction, be said of Sidney Hook. The old Yiddish proverb says it cogently: "*Vos mir zeinen, zeinen mir, ober Idn zeinen mir!*" (We are whatever we may be, but we are Jews!)

Part 2

Jurists

4

Louis Dembitz Brandeis

Louis D. Brandeis (1856-1941) was the first Jew to be appointed a Justice of the United States Supreme Court. His work as a jurist made him one of the three or four most important Justices in the history of the Supreme Court. In 1911, five years before his appointment, he became interested in Jewish life and culture, and soon became actively involved in Zionist thought and work. "My approach to Zionism," he wrote, "was through Americanism . . . to be good Americans we must be better Jews, and to be better Jews we must become Zionists. Jewish life cannot be preserved and developed, assimilation cannot be averted, unless there be established in the fatherland a center from which the Jewish spirit may radiate and give to the Jews scattered throughout the world that inspiration which springs from the memories of a great past and the hope of a great future." In 1914 he became chairman of what in effect was the World Zionist Organization, and he continued in his leadership position to 1921. The Palestine (now Israel) Endowment Fund that he founded and to which he contributed generously still administers millions of dollars for the support of important Israeli projects. In 1918 he was a co-founder of the American Jewish Congress.

*   *   *

In 1654 a tiny vessel, the St. Charles, deposited twenty-three Jews in New York, the Dutch colony on the Hudson. While individual Jews had probably arrived earlier, the landing of this group marked the beginning of Jewish immigration to the United States. By 1848 the

Jewish population was about twenty thousand, most of them immigrants from Western Europe. Some of these men and women, touched by the Emancipation and the Enlightenment, came because the failure of the 1848 revolution in Central Europe had convinced them that only in the United States would they find freedom and equality of opportunity.

Among the "Forty-Eighters" was Adolph Brandeis, a native of Prague, who would have fought in the 1848 revolution had he not been stricken by typhoid fever. Instead, in the fall of that year, he migrated to the United States. Adolph, fascinated by America, promptly applied for naturalization. "I already love our country so much," he wrote to Frederika Dembitz, his fiancee, "that I rejoice when I can sing its praises." In 1849 the steamship *Washington* brought twenty-six members of the Brandeis, Dembitz, and Wehle families. Adolph and Frederika were soon married, and settled in Madison, Indiana; after two years they moved to Louisville, Kentucky, where their son Louis Dembitz was born on November 13, 1856.

Adolph Brandeis prospered as a grain merchant. After Louis graduated from high school, the family went to Europe for three years, part of which time Louis spent at school in Dresden. When they returned to the United States, Louis, then nineteen, entered Harvard Law School, and achieved a scholastic record for excellence that became a legend. On graduation Brandeis went to St. Louis, but two years later he opened a law office in Boston in partnership with Samuel D. Warren, Jr., a former classmate at Harvard. The firm did well. At the age of twenty-six Brandeis was successful in raising a fund sufficient to install Oliver Wendell Holmes, Jr., in a law professorship at Harvard Law School. At about the same time he himself accepted an invitation to teach a course in legal evidence at Harvard, but the next year refused the offer of an assistant professorship—he preferred to remain in active law practice. He organized the Harvard Law School Association, and for this as well as other notable contributions to his alma mater, Harvard awarded him an M.A. degree in 1891. By this time he enjoyed an annual income of fifty thousand dollars—a fabulous amount at that time (by 1907 Brandeis had earned a million dollars, and ten years later was a millionaire twice over). His reputation as a leading corporation lawyer was firmly established.[1]

Brandeis' financial independence enabled him to work without compensation for public causes that interested him. Early in life he had begun to seek out such causes, and soon many such causes sought him. He was a rare phenomenon: a successful business lawyer with a keen social conscience and an irrepressible desire to work for a better world. He became the model for the later public interest lawyers and consumer interest advocates. Although never opposed to capitalism, Brandeis was one of the first successful Americans to propose measures against the social and moral abuses of aggressive capitalism. He was among the first also to insist on representation of the public interest at legislative hearings.[2]

Early Concern with Social Problems

Brandeis pioneered for the idea of collective bargaining between employers and labor unions. He maintained that unions should not be branded and persecuted as criminal conspiracies; big business made big unions necessary. If unions acted arbitrarily, unreasonably, or criminally, their evil acts or tendencies should be repressed, but their existence and legitimate interests should be encouraged and protected. As early as 1911 he favored legislation restricting the use of the injunction in labor disputes. Earlier in 1904, he had urged stabilization and full employment policies. He had advised management to open its books for inspection by unions so that a proper factual basis for collective bargaining with respect to wages could be established, thus anticipating a decision of the Supreme Court made in 1960.[3] He saw the labor unions as a great conservative force, a bulwark against radicalism and socialism. Though he opposed the closed shop as a restriction on the rights of workers, he favored a union in every shop. The right to combine, he maintained, was absolute, even among public employees; the right to strike, however, was not absolute. In sum. Brandeis was a pathfinder: he projected social policies that later were embodied in the Norris-LaGuardia Act of 1932, the Wagner Act of 1935, the Employment Act of 1946, and the Taft-Hartley Act of 1947.[4]

According to Brandeis himself, it was the Homestead Strike of 1892 that set him to thinking seriously about the labor problem. At Homestead, Pennsylvania, the scene of one of the most bitterly fought labor disputes in American history, the manager of one of the largest steel plants in the United States had hired about three hundred men of the Pinkerton private detective agency to protect company property as well as the non-union men who had been hired during the strike. An armed battle broke out between the Pinkerton men and the strikers in which sixty men were wounded and ten killed. The governor of Pennsylvania called out the National Guard, under whose protection the company kept the non-union employees at work and broke the strike. It took the shock of that battle, said Brandeis, "to turn my mind definitely toward a searching study of the relations of labor to industry."[5] While other American leaders were also shocked by the happenings at Homestead, Brandeis was one of the very few who proceeded to study the causes of the evil and search for remedies.

Brandeis also tackled other pressing social problems. He exposed the industrial life insurance racket and agitated on behalf of insurance by savings banks instead of by insurance companies. (Three states— Massachusetts, Connecticut, and New York—have since enacted laws that permit the Brandeis form of insurance.[6]) Indeed, whenever he had an opportunity, Brandeis fought against monopolies. He saw a threat to the average person in the large trusts, holding companies, cartels, interlocking corporate directorships—in big business in general. Without economic opportunity and economic democracy for individuals, Brandeis argued, political democracy would be ineffective. He therefore raised his voice against every form of absolutism, whether in government, business, or organized labor. He did not consider monopolies a necessary evil that should or could be regulated by government, and opposed regulated monopoly; he wanted instead regulated competition among business and industrial units that would not engage in monopolistic practices.[7]

Contribution to American Labor History

In the first several decades of the twentieth century both the employers and workers in the garment industry in New York City were predominantly Jewish immigrants. The International Ladies' Garment Workers' Union was demanding the closed shop while the employers attacked the union as a Marxist conspiracy. A state of anarchy existed. In 1910 there was a general strike that engendered much bitterness on both sides. Neither party was willing to make concessions or consider compromises. Following the intervention of certain civic leaders, all agreed that the only hope of bringing the dispute to an end lay in empowering Brandeis to confer with both labor and management and submit a plan of negotiation.

This was done; and it is related that in the course of the bitter arguments between garment workers and their "bosses," Brandeis at times heard a man shout in Yiddish: "*Ihr darft sich shemen! Passt dos far a Idn?*" ("Shame! Is this worthy of a Jew?") On one occasion he heard a shopworker confront his employer with a quotation in Hebrew from the prophet Isaiah:

> It is you who have devoured the vineyard, the spoil of the poor
>   is in your houses.
> What do you mean by crushing My people, by grinding the face
>   of the poor? Says the Lord God of hosts.[8]

Brandeis was deeply moved by such incidents.

At Brandeis' insistence, the union waived the closed shop, which led to a temporary split in the ranks of the workers. At a peace conference of union representatives and employers, Brandeis stated that his interest was not only in getting them to reach an accord that would end the strike, but also, and of greater significance, to create a relationship that would make future strikes unnecessary. As the basis for industrial peace, Brandeis proposed the preferential union shop, whereby the employer would have the right to select employees on the basis of their qualifications, but with preference for qualified union members. Union shop standards were to prevail in the industry. This proposal was attacked by extremists as a sell-out to the other side. After months of wrangling and negotiations, the protocol, as Brandeis called it, was accepted and signed by all concerned.

This agreement has played a notable role in American labor history as one of the first important collective bargaining agreements. It marked, on the one hand, a departure by organized labor from its persistent demand for total union security, that is, the closed shop, and, on the other hand, a departure by employers from their obstinate refusal to concede recognition to labor unions. The protocol also introduced into a disorganized industry a form of self-policing and self-government by setting up an inspection board to standardize and maintain proper working conditions. The protocol also proceeded on the principle, now universally followed, that the agreement is only the initial step in achieving and maintaining industrial peace and democracy; accordingly, it provided for a grievance board with authority to settle disputes arising out of the agreement; if this agency failed to achieve a dispute settlement, the grievance was to be submitted to a board of arbitrators. Lockouts and strikes were not to take place. For its day, the introduction of arbitration for the settlement of grievances was a pioneering step—one which set the pattern for the future.

Efforts for Scientific Management

Shortly after the protocol was signed, Brandeis turned his attention to scientific management, which attracted national attention to the inefficient methods prevailing in American industry. At the end of 1910 the Interstate Commerce Commission conducted public hearings on proposed increases in railroad freight charges. Brandeis, testifying on behalf of the public interest, opposed the increases on the ground that the public should not be compelled to subsidize the inefficient operation of the carriers. Brandeis charged the railroads with engaging in practices that victimized the consumer and the small businessman—particularly, increasing rates constantly in order to meet higher costs. With scientific management, Brandeis maintained, the carriers could pay higher wages without raising rates. By introducing efficiency methods, he argued, they could add a million dollars a day to their income.

These statements by Brandeis created a sensation, and the subjects of business efficiency and scientific management were widely discussed by the public for the first time. Though the railroads attacked Brandeis, within a decade industrialists, including railroad executives, admitted the legitimacy of his claims on behalf of the application of scientific methods to industrial management.

What seemed radical in the first decade of the twentieth century has since become an accepted truth. Just as he worked to make industrial management scientific, Brandeis also sought for ways to make business a profession. In this effort, too, he was a pioneer: today schools of business administration are integral divisions of many universities throughout the country.

In these various ways, Brandeis contributed greatly to an awareness and understanding of social problems. One can easily see his influence in the policies of Samuel Gompers, Sidney Hillman, David Dubinsky, Walter Reuther, and other leaders of American organized labor. Brandeis helped direct American thought and institutions away from the class-struggle ideologies and toward union-employer cooperation, expressed in collective bargaining agreements and in basic social legislation. Not utopianism, but constant improvement through practical measures was the aim of Brandeis's reformism—a philosophy he derived from Benjamin Franklin, Jefferson, Emerson, and William James, which eventually linked itself with the New Freedom, the New Deal, and the Fair Deal.

Contribution to American Law

Notable and enduring as was Brandeis's impact on American liberal thought and the country's social and economic institutions, his contribution to American law and legal institutions was even greater. In his work as a legal reformer he was, on the whole, a solitary pathfinder: his work was daring and original. And here, too, his effort was not to destroy but to preserve and to give new direction and new life.

In 1908 Brandeis introduced the economic or "Brandeis" brief into the Supreme Court, an act of adventurous courage which alone would have won him distinction in American jurisprudence. In *Muller v. Oregon*[9] the Supreme Court had before it a state statute that limited to ten the number of hours for women workers. At the request of the State of Oregon, Brandeis wrote the brief in defense of the statute, devoting most of it to economic and statistical data and to arguments drawn from official reports which showed that long hours of work were dangerous to women's health, morals, and welfare. This approach—putting the main weight of the argument on economic and sociological factual studies, rather than on dry logic or a priori arguments—was bold and new. No lawyer had ever before dared to argue a law case in this way. The Supreme Court was won over by Brandeis and his brief: the Oregon statute was held to be constitutional, and the court openly complimented Brandeis for bringing before it facts and opinions showing that the act was not unreasonable.

After this sensational success, Brandeis continued to file similar briefs in state and federal cases; a pattern was thus established that lawyers and judges no longer question. The later struggle to validate, constitutionally, social legislation enacted by Congress and by the state legislatures, which was won in 1937, when the Supreme Court began to uphold New Deal legislation,[10] could never have been resolved were it not for the deep and pervasive influence of the Brandeis approach to constitutional questions affecting social legislation. The

American people enjoy today the fruit of ideas planted by Brandeis as far back as 1908.

Justice of the Supreme Court

It was against the background of such monumental achievements that Brandeis was nominated for the United States Supreme Court by President Woodrow Wilson early in 1916. Since he was the first Jew to receive this honor, the conservative forces in the country were aroused: seven former presidents of the American Bar Association, including William Howard Taft, opposed confirmation; so, too, did A. Lawrence Lowell, president of Harvard University (although Brandeis was a Harvard Law School overseer at the time). But Charles W. Eliot, Harvard's president emeritus, favored Brandeis; so did Newton D. Baker, who became secretary of war in March 1916, and Frances Perkins, who was to become Franklin D. Roosevelt's secretary of labor. In the Senate committee named to consider the nomination, ten Democrats voted for and eight Republicans voted against confirmation. After five months of public controversy, the appointment was approved in the Senate by a vote of 47 to 22.[11]

Brandeis was sixty years of age when he took his place on the Supreme Court. He retired in 1939 after twenty-three years of distinguished service. His name and his record stand with those of John Marshall, Joseph Story, Stephen J. Field, Oliver Wendell Holmes, and Benjamin N. Cardozo.

A major contribution of Justice Brandeis was to deepen public consciousness of the significance of civil liberties. With Justice Holmes, Brandeis worked incessantly to teach his colleagues and the American people that unless basic human freedoms were respected, protected, and strengthened, American society and institutions would hardly be worthy of a notable place in the history of mankind. This conviction was expressed by Holmes and Brandeis consistently and repeatedly, most of the time in dissenting opinions, some of which have become important historic documents.[12]

In a case before the Court in 1919, Justice Holmes first formulated the clear and present danger doctrine; it remained, however, for Justice Brandeis to give the clearest articulation of this doctrine in an opinion he wrote in 1927.[13] The fundamental freedoms enumerated in the First Amendment, he said, may not be denied or abridged; yet the freedoms of speech and assembly that were involved in the case are not absolutes. They may be restricted by necessity, but constitutionally the necessity does not exist "unless speech would produce, or is intended to produce, a clear and imminent danger of some substantive evil which the state constitutionally may seek to prevent." When a state enacts a law to meet an evil, and the law limits the exercise of a fundamental liberty, it is the duty of the Court to determine for itself whether the enactment was in fact necessary; the Court is not bound by the fact that the vast majority of a state's citizens believe that the dissemination of certain doctrines is fraught with evil consequences. At one time, said Brandeis, "man feared witches and burned women. It is the function of speech to free men from the bondage of irrational fears." To justify, constitutionally, restrictions on free speech, said Brandeis, there must be "reasonable ground to fear that serious evil will result if free speech is practiced; reasonable ground to believe that the danger apprehended is imminent; reasonable ground to believe that the evil to be prevented is a serious one."

The clear and present danger doctrine, as stated by Holmes and Brandeis in numerous opinions, has become an accepted constitutional interpretation. Though it has not always been identified as the clear and present danger test, and although it has not always been followed, even those who attack or question its force do not disregard it. The doctrine stands as a "fence" to protect the First Amendment freedoms against attempts to whittle them down in the name of alleged national security or state emergencies. To all persons who would play fast and loose with these freedoms, the words of Brandeis stand as a reminder and a warning: "Those who won our independence by revolution were not cowards. They did not fear political change. They did not exalt order at the cost of liberty."[14]

Brandeis's second most notable contribution as a justice of the Supreme Court was his insistence that Congress and the states have constitutionally the discretion to experiment with economic and social institutions in the light of facts that show a need for action. While a clear and present danger—and only such a danger—may justify an abridgment of a fundamental liberty, much more freedom is vested in the legislative judgment as it is brought to bear on economic and social problems. There is no right to experiment with human rights, but there is a right to experiment with economic and social institutions. It is, said Brandeis, "one of the happy incidents of the federal system that a single courageous state may, if its citizens choose, serve as a laboratory, and try novel social and economic experiments without risk to the rest of the country."[15] As long as the statute setting up the social experiment is not arbitrary, capricious, or unreasonable, the United States Constitution should not be interpreted to stand in the way.

The same open-mindedness for which Brandeis pleaded in his economic brief submitted to the Court in *Muller v. Oregon* appears in his work as a Supreme Court justice, mainly, however, in his dissenting opinions (with which Justice Holmes generally agreed). The scientific attitude, he argued, must be permitted application to social and economic problems faced by the nation and the states. The advances in science have shown that what seems to be impossible sometimes happens. The progress made in science and technology attests to the value of the trial-and-error method, the method of experimentation. The Due Process Clause of the Fourteenth Amendment, Brandeis contended, must not be used to stand in the way of efforts to improve our social institutions—and improvements can be brought about only through experiments, some of which may fail and some of which may succeed. In a dissenting opinion, Brandeis told his colleagues on the Court that to stand in the way of experimentation in social and economic matters was a grave responsibility; the denial of this right may bring about serious consequences; the right should not be denied unless the legislative measure is clearly arbitrary. The Court should not strike down a statute that seeks a solution to a difficult social problem by interjecting prejudices into legal principles. "If we would guide by the light of reason," said Brandeis, "we must let our minds be bold."[16]

The intellectual boldness to which Brandeis challenged the Court often involved the necessity to overcome prior decisions. On this point, too, Brandeis insisted that the Court must follow not precedents, but the light of reason. In constitutional cases the Court should decide either to follow a precedent or to overrule it. In overruling earlier decisions that involve constitutional provisions, said Brandeis in a dissenting opinion in 1932, the Court merely bows to the lessons of experience and to the force of better reasoning and recognizes that the process of trial and error, so fruitful in the physical sciences, is also appropriate in the judicial process. In other words, just as the legislatures may resort to the scientific method in conducting social experiments, so, too, may the courts conduct judicial experiments which entail the rejection of precedents that have not stood the test of time.[17]

The Constitution, if it is to be a living force in the affairs of men, must not be merely worshipped or venerated but used as an instrument that encourages the exercise of the free intelligence as it struggles with the complex problems of American society. It was not until 1937 that the Supreme Court was won over to the Brandeis logic and method. It was the dissenting opinions of Brandeis—and Holmes—that prepared the ground for the New Deal changes in the Supreme Court— and for the school desegregation decision in *Brown v. Topeka* in 1954.[18]

The Right of Privacy

In 1890, twenty-six years before Brandeis took his seat on the Supreme Court, he and his law partner Samuel D. Warren published an article in the *Harvard Law Review*, with the title "The Right to Privacy," that has had an influence on the development of American law that perhaps exceeds that of any other publication in a legal periodical.[19] Its impact was not felt immediately, but from the 1960s on it became possible to assert that "a more influential piece of scholarship is difficult to imagine."[20]

The article argued that recent inventions and aggressive business methods have made it necessary for the law to secure for the person what Thomas M. Cooley, in his *Treatise on the Law of Torts* (1880), referred to as "personal immunity," the "right to one's person," the "right to be let alone." The article said, "The intensity and complexity of life attendant upon advancing civilization, have rendered necessary some retreat from the world, . . . solitude and privacy have become more essential to the individual."

Although recognizing the fact that the common law and statutes accorded some personal protection that might be viewed as aspects of privacy—for example, libel and defamation law, a right to intellectual or artistic property—the article argued on behalf of a general right of privacy, "enforcement of the more general right of the individual to be let alone," "a general right to privacy for thoughts, emotions, and sensations," "the more general right to the immunity of the person,— the right to one's personality," the "right of property in its widest sense, including all possession, including all rights and privileges, and hence embracing the right to an inviolate personality."

One of the important aspects of the article is its clear moral tone, its grounding in the belief in the dignity and inviolability of the human being; the belief that the human being—any and every human being— is more than a social animal, that there is an aspect of the human being that stands outside of society, an aspect that may not be invaded by neighbors or government. This aspect of the human being is comprehended in his privacy, which the law should recognize and protect. It has been suggested that the right of privacy, as projected by the Warren-Brandeis article is ultimately grounded on natural law philosophy.[21]

It was not until 1965 that the Supreme Court, for the first time, recognized the right of privacy as constitutionally guaranteed, notwithstanding the fact that it is not expressly provided in the Constitution. A Connecticut statute made the use of contraceptives (even when used by a married couple) a criminal offense. In *Griswold v. Connecticut* [22] the Supreme Court held the act unconstitutional as an invasion of the right of privacy of married persons. In a later case, decided in 1972, the Court extended its holding to apply also to single persons.[23]

"We deal with a right of privacy," Justice William O. Douglas wrote in his opinion for the Court in *Griswold*, "older than the Bill of Rights—older than our political parties." In *Eisenstadt* the Court said, "If the right of privacy means anything, it is the right of the individual, married or single, to be free from unwarranted governmental intrusion into matters so fundamentally affecting a person as the decision whether to bear or beget a child." Then in 1973, one year after *Eisenstadt*, the Court took a further step and moved from the right to use contraceptives to the right of a woman to terminate her pregnancy. This decision—*Roe v. Wade*[24]—has generated much controversy, but the controversy is not over the constitutional right of privacy, but over its inclusion of the specific decision that the right of privacy, as the Supreme Court held, is "broad enough to encompass a woman's decision whether or not to terminate her pregnancy."

In his opinion for the Court in *Griswold* Justice Douglas enumerated certain provisions in the Constitution that guarantee specific privacy rights, like the guarantee against unreasonable searches and seizures, and then added, "Various guarantees create zones of privacy," and these "zones" in the Bill of Rights "have penumbras, formed by emanations from those guarantees that help give them life and substance." Ralph Waldo Emerson, long before the *Griswold* case, was aware of the efficacy of "emanations." "Every natural fact," wrote

Emerson, in 1841[25] "is an emanation, and that from which it ema-
nates is an emanation also, and from every emanation is a new emanation." It was the genius of Warren and Brandeis to have discovered
the "emanation" of the right to privacy, from which "emanations"
have followed, and who can foresee what others are yet to be claimed
and vindicated?

Brandeis Joins the Zionist Movement

It was characteristic of Brandeis, who demonstrated in every aspect
of his legal career a passion for social justice, that, once won to the
cause of Zionism, he would approach it on the practical, pragmatic
level, and give it the fullest measure of his devotion. In 1912, two
years after Brandeis's mediation of the ILGWU strike, Jacob de Haas,
who had been London secretary to Theodor Herzl, and was now editor
of the *Jewish Advocate* in Boston, called on Brandeis for his views on
certain aspects of savings bank insurance that might be of special
interest to Jewish parents. At one point De Haas spoke of Louis N.
Dembitz, Brandeis's uncle as a "noble Jew" and an early Zionist. De
Haas spoke also of Herzl and the Zionist movement. Brandeis was
greatly interested. Other discussions followed, which led Brandeis
to study published materials on Zionism. When he joined the Federation of American Zionists, this fact was publicly announced at
the Zionist convention in Cleveland. In 1913 Brandeis presided at
a meeting in Boston to welcome Nahum Sokolow, Zionist intellectual and leader from Europe, and he made other appearances at
Zionist meetings in different parts of the country. At the national
Zionist convention in Cincinnati in 1913, Brandeis advocated the
diversion of Jewish immigration to Palestine, negotiation with the
Turkish government (then in control of Palestine) for large concessions, and the industrialization of Palestine through capital invest-
ment.

After the outbreak of World War I in 1914, it seemed desirable to
move the world center of Zionist activities from Europe to the United
States. On August 30 of that year a New York conference of 150
Zionists was held, at which a provisional executive Committee for
General Zionist Affairs was organized. Brandeis became chairman
and thus leader of the Zionist movement in the United States at a time
of international crisis.

Chairman of Zionist Provisional Committee

At the close of the New York meeting which elected Brandeis, the administrative committee which he headed worked almost all night and the next day. Characteristically, Brandeis injected into the new task his tremendous drive, capacity for hard work, and an eagerness for facts and practical results.

In accepting the chairmanship Brandeis had told the conferees that he considered it his duty to aid the cause "so far as it is in my power to do so." He was aware of his own "disqualifications" for the important task:

> Throughout long years which represent my life [he was then fifty-eight], I have been to a great extent separated from Jews. I am very ignorant in things Jewish. But recent experiences, public and professional, have taught me this: I find Jews possessed of those very qualities which we of the twentieth century seek to develop in our struggle for justice and democracy; a deep moral feeling which makes them capable of noble acts; a deep sense of the brotherhood of man; and a high intelligence, the fruit of three-thousand years of civilization.

> These experiences have made me feel that the Jewish people have something which should be saved for the world; that the Jewish people should be preserved; and that it is our duty to pursue that method of saving which most promises success.[26]

In his position as leader of Zionism in the United States, Brandeis subsequently traveled to many cities, where he delivered lectures which were heard by thousands of persons and were read in printed form by many additional thousands. He made a special point of answering the charge of some anti-Zionists that Zionism was disloyalty to America. Zionism "is not a movement to remove all the Jews compulsorily to Palestine," Brandeis pointed out. Zionism was a movement to enlarge—and not to contract—the freedom of the Jews so that, like the Greek, the Irish, or the German, he might exercise an option to live in the land of his fathers or in another country of his choice. By supporting Zionism, an American Jew was not necessarily seeking to change his own home, but rather to win for Jews everywhere the freedom to make their home in Palestine or elsewhere. For Jews who did not wish to leave the United States, a Jewish state in Palestine would serve as a center from which Jewish values radiate and as a spiritual force to preserve Jews from assimilation; it would give Jews everywhere "that inspiration which springs from memories of a great past and the hope of a great future."

Brandeis brought this same message to audiences of young people at Harvard, Columbia, and other universities. In 1915 he wrote that "Zionist affairs are really the important things in life now." Not a day went by that he did not do some work on behalf of the cause. He insisted on frequent and detailed reports from the Zionist organization staff—no detail was too small for his interest. He sought opportunities to address groups hostile to Zionism so that he might win them over. He was deeply moved by the disclosures of wholesale miseries suffered by Jews in Russia and Poland, and in his speeches he appealed for funds, linking relief and Zionism, the immediate needs and the future hopes of the Jewish people.

Anticipating the end of the war and settlement of international political questions, Zionist leaders in Europe and the United States prepared themselves to place before the Allied Powers definite demands with respect to Palestine as well as for equal rights for all European Jews. Since Brandeis thought it essential to unite American Jewry, early in 1916 he joined in a call for a democratically constituted American Jewish congress, to help win Jewish rights in Palestine and the rights of Jews in other countries. Twenty-six organizations agreed to establish this congress. Brandeis was temporary chairman and honorary president. Just at that time he was confirmed as associate justice of the Supreme Court, and he felt it necessary to resign from these positions. Though he cut all his other ties with social causes and organizations, his Zionist work, however, did not cease.[27]

Balfour Declaration

As a justice of the Supreme Court, Brandeis enjoyed even more prestige than he had in the past; and this increased his usefulness for Zionist ends. Zionist leaders everywhere were intent on winning a settlement of the Palestine question as part of the over-all peace settlement that was to follow the end of World War I. In 1914 Brandeis had discussed the Palestine question with President Wilson and later with the British and French ambassadors to the United States, and in the next few years he continued discussions and negotiations with the Department of State and Allied officials. On April 6, 1917, the United States entered the war, which facilitated negotiations with regard to

Palestine. In May 1917, Brandeis met Lord Balfour, foreign secretary in Lloyd George's coalition ministry, at the White House, where the latter had come as head of Britain's war mission. Balfour had expressed his eagerness to see Brandeis, and later Brandeis conferred with both Wilson and Balfour. He was also in close contact with Zionist leaders in Britain, notably Chaim Weizmann and James Rothschild.

On November 2, 1917, the Balfour Declaration was issued, pledging British support for the establishment in Palestine of a national home for the Jewish people. At the 1918 Zionist convention, held in Pittsburgh, Brandeis offered a five-point social justice code for Palestine, which was adopted and became known as the Pittsburgh Program. It called for political and civil equality of all inhabitants without regard to creed, race, or sex; public ownership and control of the land and its natural resources and all public utilities; the leasing of land on conditions that would insure fullest opportunity for development and continuity of possession; the setting up of all economic institutions on the cooperative principle; and a system of free public schools.[28] Since American Zionists supported these principles, but European Zionists resisted making them part of the Zionist policy for and in Palestine, the two groups began to drift apart.

Brandeis and Weizmann

On November 11, 1918, the war came to an end. The following year Brandeis travelled to London, where he met Weizmann for the first time. In his autobiography, *Trial and Error*, Weizmann described his impression of Brandeis as follows:

> Justice Brandeis has often been compared with Abraham Lincoln, and indeed they had much in common besides clean-chiseled features and lofty brows. Brandeis, too, was a Puritan: upright, austere, of a scrupulous honesty and implacable logic. These qualities sometimes made him hard to work with; like Wilson, he was apt to evolve theories, based on the highest principles, from his inner consciousness, and then expect the facts to fit in with them. If the facts failed to oblige, so much the worse for the facts. Indeed, the conflicts which developed between Brandeis and ourselves were not unlike those which disturbed Wilson's relations with his European colleagues when he first had to work closely with them.[29]

Weizmann thought of Brandeis as a doctrinaire theoretician whose mind worked from premise to fact; this was, however, a complete misconception because actually the mind of Brandeis worked in just the opposite way, from fact to concept. In truth, Brandeis was the least doctrinaire of men; his hunger for facts was insatiable, and he searched them out without fixed preconceptions.

After Brandeis left London, he went to Paris to confer with Wilson, Balfour, and others; he then travelled to Palestine, where he visited all the cities and most of the colonies. This trip confirmed his belief that Palestine must become the Jewish homeland.

The following year (1920), a World Zionist conference was held in London. Weizmann was elected president; Brandeis, head of the American delegation, was named honorary president. But it was apparent that these two men did not agree on fundamental policies, and that a break between them was inevitable. In Brandeis's view, the future called for practical work in Palestine: acquisition of more land, reforestation, public health, immigration, capital investments. He wanted men with business and executive abilities to take over the main portion of the work, and he was prepared to welcome the cooperation of non-Zionists in the practical work of building up the land. To Weizmann, however, political Zionists still had important functions to perform; the Balfour Declaration and the acceptance by Great Britain of the mandate over Palestine in April 1920 were only the start of a new era of Zionist political work and political action. Weizmann did not want to see Zionist forces compromised in any way by non-Zionists working within the organization. When Weizmann's views prevailed at the London conference, Brandeis resigned as honorary president.

The Cleveland Convention

In time Brandeis also lost the support of most American Zionists. In 1921 the Zionist Organization of America met in Cleveland, and Weizmann came over to attend the convention. Brandeis's administration lost on a vote of confidence; he resigned as leader but refused to lead a secessionist movement or leave the organization. Thereafter he devoted much time and energy to those Palestine agencies that had undertaken practical tasks in the rebuilding of the land.

As later years demonstrated, Weizmann had been right in thinking that the political activities of Zionist organizations had much work to accomplish before Palestine would in fact become the national homeland. But Brandeis had also been correct in stressing the practical work that needed to be done. Perhaps if each had accepted the other's point of view without relinquishing his own, Zionism would have made much faster strikes, both practically and politically, during the period from 1921 to 1948.

Even after Brandeis had ceased to be an official leader of the Zionist forces, he continued until the end of his life to give the movement his moral and financial support. At the time of his death, the residue of his large estate, beyond what was willed to his immediate family, was divided as follows: one-fourth to Survey Associates for the maintenance of civil liberty and the promotion of workers' education, one-fourth for the library and law school of the University of Louisville, and the remaining one-half for "the upbuilding of Palestine as a national home for the Jewish people."[30]

Brandeis's Zionist Philosophy

What did Zionism mean to Brandeis? Why did "the upbuilding of Palestine as a national home for the Jewish people" have such a profound hold on his mind and heart?

First, he saw the Jewish homeland as a small country, free of the curse of bigness. Being small, it could conduct daring experiments in social living and social justice, and the citizens would be able quickly and effectively to judge of the success or failure of their new ventures.

Second, Brandeis felt that given the character of the Jewish pioneers in Palestine, the new settlement would be an almost pure democracy, with women and men equal partners in economic and political rights and activities. In the colonies, economic differences, if they existed, were not to serve as a basis for the enjoyment or denial of political and economic democracy or the rights and duties flowing from democracy. Brandeis was certain that the ideals of freedom and equality would flourish in the Jewish homeland, and lead to extraordinary spiritual and social developments. Third, Brandeis sensed that in the Jewish homeland the settlers would enjoy the fundamental right to be different, to be themselves. A people, no less than a person, he felt, has the right to mold and order its life in its own way, expressing its own genius, ideals, history, and traditions. The Jews collectively should enjoy the rights and freedoms to develop as do other groups of people. In Palestine, Brandeis stated, Jews would enjoy not only the personal rights and freedoms they should have as citizens of any democratic state, but, in addition, they would also enjoy group rights and freedoms, to develop their own language, ways of thought and living.

By achieving these group rights and freedoms in their own homeland. Jews could make an important contribution to their co-religionists living elsewhere. The American Jew would thus benefit from the development of Jewish culture in the homeland. Furthermore, like all other peoples, American Jews should have the option to remain in the United States or go to Palestine. The establishment of a Jewish homeland would thus give Jews everywhere freedoms hitherto denied them by the tragedies of their history—freedom, of choice, freedom to be different, and freedom to enjoy spiritual ties with their own people.

The Jewish nation in Palestine would be different, for the Jewish settlers there would bring to a common center qualities of character and moral and social ideals that were the fruit of their history, tradition, and experience. Brandeis put high among those qualities and ideals the reverence for law and the concept of morality. He also included commitments to brotherhood and righteousness, democratic and cooperative living, social justice, and peace. Further characteristics were, in his view, a strong sense of duty and right, high intellectual attainments based on the belief in universal education, and a strong sense of community responsibility.

"Such is our inheritance," said Justice Brandeis; "such the estate which we hold in trust." What obligations are imposed by this trust?

> The short answer is noblesse oblige; and its command is twofold. It imposes duties upon us in respect to our own conduct as individuals; it imposes no less important duties upon us as part of the Jewish community or people. Self-respect demands that each of us lead individually a life worthy of our great inheritance and of the glorious traditions of the people. But this is demanded also by respect for the rights of others. The Jews have not only been ever known as a "peculiar people" they were and remain a distinctive and minority people. Now it is one of the necessary incidents of a distinctive and minority people that the act of any one is in some degree attributed to the whole group. A single though inconspicuous instance of dishonorable conduct on the part of a Jew in any trade or profession has far-reaching evil effects extending to the many innocent members of the race. Large as this country is, no Jew can behave badly without injuring each of us in the end. . . . Since the act of each becomes thus the concern of all, we are perforce our brothers' keepers, exacting even from the lowliest the avoidance of things dishonorable; and we may properly brand the guilty as disloyal to the people. . . .

> And yet, though the Jew makes his individual life the loftiest, that alone will not fulfill the obligations of his trust. We are bound not only to use worthily

our great inheritance, but to preserve, and if possible, augment it; and then transmit it to coming generations. The fruit of three thousand years of civilization and a hundred generations of suffering may not be sacrificed by us. It will be sacrificed if dissipated. Assimilation is national suicide. And assimilation can be prevented only by preserving national characteristics and life as other peoples, large and small, are preserving and developing their national life. Shall we with our inheritance do less than the Irish? . . . And must we not, like them, have a land where the Jewish life may be naturally led, the Jewish language spoken, and the Jewish spirit prevail? Surely we must, and that land is our fathers' land; it is Palestine.[31]

Adapting a phrase of Mazzini, Justice Brandeis said that no Jew may be a moral mediocrity. And that, he added, was precisely how the Jewish pioneers in Palestine felt because they were conscious of their inheritance. "It is the Jewish tradition," Brandeis said, "and the Jewish law, and the Jewish spirit which prepare us for the lessons of life. In Palestine the younger generation is taught that heritage and as a result they live for the highest and the best of what life is and what it may be."

Finally, Brandeis saw in Zionism the possibility for the American Jew of living and thinking in a pluralistic world. A free man who seeks spiritual riches must have many loyalties. "Multiple loyalties," said Brandeis, "are objectionable only if they are inconsistent. . . . Every American Jew who aids in advancing the Jewish settlement in Palestine, though he feels that neither he nor his descendants will ever live there, will . . . be a better American for doing so."

Zionism and Americanism Compatible

Since "the twentieth-century ideals of America have been the ideals of the Jew for more than twenty centuries," and Zionism is committed to the preservation and strengthening of these ideals in Jewish living in a Jewish homeland, it followed for Brandeis that "to be good Americans, we must become Zionists." The Jewish rebuilding in Palestine, furthermore, would enable American Jews better to perform their duty to the United States, for it would help them to make "toward the attainment of the American ideals of democracy and social justice that large contribution for which religion and life have peculiarly fitted the Jew." "The Zionist ideals, the highest Jewish ideals," Brandeis said, "are essentially the American ideals."

Thus, with a logic that is unanswerable and with a conviction that went to the deep recesses of his heart and soul, Brandeis found in

Zionism a home for all his important values and ideals, both Jewish and American—for his faith in freedom and democracy, his love of experimentation, his pluralistic philosophy, his social conscience, his prophetic commitment to righteousness and justice, his strong sense of group loyalty, his belief in equality and in the right of the person and the group to be different.

In an opinion he wrote in 1927, Brandeis said that "the greatest menace to freedom is an inert people."[32] While in saying this he had in mind the American people and American civil liberties, Brandeis could have applied the same thought to the Jewish people. In Zionism, Brandeis saw a way to maximize the living forces in Judaism and in the Jewish people: free acts on behalf of freedom.

Conclusion

How can one summarize a life such as Brandeis's? He was an enemy of bigness, yet he himself was big, very big. His life left us a great legacy. He taught us a number of very significant lessons.

The late Professor Paul Freund, who had clerked for Justice Brandeis, observed that Brandeis was able to see moral issues "in what others saw as vast, impersonal, inevitable trends."[33] This was, indeed, an important aspect of the mind and temper of Brandeis. To see a moral dimension in a situation takes a special sensitivity, that needs to be cultivated and nurtured, like seeing an aesthetic aspect to a phenomenon when others are blind or deaf.

But more than this was involved, as Freund went on to say, for Brandeis had the genius to "devise institutional arrangements designed to salvage moral values in a modern technological age." And so Brandeis designed life insurance sold by savings banks; he projected collective bargaining between unions and employers; he pioneered to protect personal privacy; he gave leadership to a Zionist movement as an answer to Jewish homelessness. These are only examples of his moral sensitivity and his practical genius.

A great contribution was the lesson he taught American judges and lawyers to concentrate on facts, facts, facts, and not to believe that empty abstractions can achieve just results. For this contribution alone Brandeis has earned a place among the top four or five leading American jurists.

Notes

1. Alpheus T. Mason, *Brandeis: A Free Man's Life* (New York, 1946), 103.
2. Ibid., p. 125.
3. *NLRB v. Truitt Mfg. Co.*, 351 U.S. 149 (1956).
4. Mason, *Brandeis*, 142, 146, 149-150.
5. Ibid., p. 87.
6. Ibid., p. 176.
7. For a full study of the savings bank life insurance plan, see A.T. Mason, *The Brandeis Way* (Princeton, 1938).
8. Isaiah 3:14-15.
9. *Muller v. Oregon*, 208 U.S. 412 (1908).
10. *NLRB v. Jones & Laughlin Steel Corp.*, 301 U.S. 1 (1937); *Steward Machine Co. v. Davis*, 301 U.S. 548 (1937).
11. Mason, *Brandeis*, chs. 30, 31.
12. For some of the opinions of Brandeis, see Alfred Lief, ed., *The Social and Economic Views of Mr. Justice Brandeis* (New York, 1930).
13. Concurring opinion in *Whitney v. Calif.*, 274 U.S. 357 (1927).
14. Ibid. cf. *Dennis v. U.S.* 341 U.S. 494, 510 (1951).
15. Dissenting opinion in *New State Ice Co. v. Liebman*, 285 U.S. 262 (1932), at 311.
16. Ibid.
17. Dissenting opinion in *Burnet v. Coronado Oil & Gas Co.,* 285 U.S. 393 (1932).
18. *Brown v. Board of Education*, 347 U.S. 483 (1954).
19. 4 *Harvard Law Rev.* 193 (1890).
20. R.C. Turkington, G.B. Trubow, A.L. Allen, eds., *Privacy Cases and Materials* (Houston, 1992), 31.
21. Ibid., p. 31.
22. *Griswold v. Conn.*, 381 U.S. 479 (1963).
23. *Eisenstadt v. Baird*, 92 S. Ct. 1029 (1972).
24. *Roe v. Wade*, 410 U.S. 113 (1973).
25. Ralph Waldo Emerson, "The Method of Nature."
26. Solomon Goldman, *The Words of Justice Brandeis* (New York, 1953), 108, 109; S. Goldman, *Brandeis on Zionism* (New York, 1942), 13.
27. Mason, *Brandeis*, 451.
28. Ibid., 454-455.
29. Chaim Weizmann, *Trial and Error* (Philadelphia, 1949), I, 248.
30. Mason, *Brandeis*, 639.
31. Goldman, *The Words of Justice Brandeis*, 184-185; Goldman, *Brandeis on Zionism*, 28.
32. Case cited supra note 13.
33. Paul Freund, "Justice Brandeis: A Law Clerk's Remembrance," *American Jewish History* 68 (9/78) 7.

5

Benjamin Nathan Cardozo

I

Among American legal scholars there is, I think, agreement that in the last two centuries of American history the five greatest jurists have been John Marshall, Oliver Wendell Holmes, Jr., Louis D. Brandeis, Benjamin Nathan Cardozo, and Learned Hand. Scholars would find it difficult, perhaps impossible, to name a sixth, for the distance between the aforementioned jurists and the next one would be too great. Marshall, Holmes, and Brandeis achieved their greatness as justices of the United States Supreme Court; Hand, as judge of the United States Court of Appeals, and Cardozo as judge of the New York Court of Appeals. Learned Hand never made it to the Supreme Court, but his firmly established fame shows that he did not need the court; the court, however, could well have used him. Cardozo was a justice of the Supreme Court only a mere five and one-half years, where he wrote only a few important opinions that only confirmed his preeminence. Holmes and Cardozo also achieved early fame for their significant contributions to jurisprudence, Holmes for his *Common Law* (1881), Cardozo for his *The Nature of the Judicial Process* (1921), each a recognized classic. The book by Cardozo is the very first book ever by a judge who analyzed the process of judging.

*   *   *

Cardozo was born in 1870 in New York City. His parents were Sephardic Jews who traced their ancestry to immigrants who came to

85

the United States in colonial times, and were closely related to the Nathans, to an ancestor Benjamin Mendes Seixas, who participated in the American Revolution, and to the Lazarus family (Emma Lazarus was a cousin). Prominent rabbis, scholars, and merchants were related to the Cardozos and were officers of Congregation Shearith Israel, the leading Sephardic, Spanish-Portuguese synagogue. Cardozo's father, Albert, was a successful lawyer, who was elected a justice of the New York Supreme Court, but resigned four years later rather than face impeachment for bribery.

Benjamin Cardozo attended Columbia College, where he was influenced by his professor of philosophy, Nicholas Murray Butler, who later became president of Columbia. While studying law at Columbia Law School, Cardozo simultaneously took graduate courses in philosophy and received the M.A. degree. After passing the bar examinations, he entered his brother's law office. Despite the disgrace that besotted the Cardozo name, Benjamin Cardozo became a successful lawyer; he enjoyed an active, lucrative litigation and appellate practice. He became known as a lawyer's lawyer, a specialist in preparing briefs for other lawyers and arguing cases before the Court of Appeals, the state's highest court. He was widely recognized by the bench and bar for his wide learning, his analytical, logical mind, and his ability as an advocate.

In 1914, when he was forty-four years of age, and after enjoying the private practice of the law for twenty-three years, he agreed to run for election as a justice of the New York Supreme Court and was elected by a narrow margin. He had not been in politics but was offered a place on the ballot because the politicians wanted to balance the ticket with a Jewish lawyer who was known to be a member of the Spanish-Portuguese congregation. His biographer claims that Cardozo chose to run for the judgeship because his father had resigned from such a position in disgrace, and he wanted to clear the Cardozo name.[1] Five weeks after he took his place on the bench, the governor designated him to sit on the Court of Appeals to help clean up a backlog of cases. He continued to serve in that court for several years when, in 1917, he was elected a judge of the court. Seven years later he was elected chief judge of the Court of Appeals. He was a judge for eighteen years and made the Court of Appeals outstanding, the most highly regarded state court in the United States, and Cardozo became the most famous and most esteemed state judge in the country. In 1932

President Herbert Hoover nominated him as associate justice of the United States Supreme Court, where he served for five and one-half years. He died in 1938, after having practiced law for twenty-three years and serving as a judge a total of twenty-four years.

Cardozo never married. He and his sister Nellie (Ellie), who was ten years his senior and who also never married, lived together until her death in 1929, when he was nearly sixty. She meant more to him than anyone else. Her death was an irreparable loss; a year after her death he wrote that there was hardly "a vacant moment when I do not think of her with love and gratitude."[2] Cardozo had many friends and relatives, but his private practice and then his court work absorbed most of his time and thought. During the eighteen years that he served on the Court of Appeals he wrote 556 opinions for the court and sixteen dissenting opinions, and unlike judges today, he did his own research and wrote his own opinions—in long-hand. On average per year he wrote thirty majority opinions, and one concurring and one dissenting opinions, and often he wrote an opinion for the conference of the judges.[3] When he became associate justice of the Supreme Court, he was the junior member for almost his full (but brief) term, and so the chief justice assigned him very few interesting, important cases, of which at least one case has left its mark.

Cardozo is famous not only for the substance of many of his opinions, but also for his literary craftsmanship. Professor Richard A. Posner, in his book *Law and Literature*, refers to Cardozo as "the most mannered of the great judicial stylists."[4] I question the appropriateness of the use of the adjective "mannered," but I doubt if any student of legal opinions will question that Cardozo was one of the great legal stylists. In this respect he is comparable to John Marshall and Justice Holmes. His eminence as a literary stylist may, in part, be attributed to the fact that, like Holmes, Cardozo was a great reader, with a remarkable photographic memory. His mind was full of literary echoes. He knew the Bible, he had read the great philosophical works by Aristotle, Plato, Schopenhauer, as well as works by his contemporaries, among them George Santayana and Alfred North Whitehead, and he had read great literary classics, including Shakespeare, Homer, Dante, Milton, Addison and Steele, and countless others.[5] He could read Greek and Latin. His knowledge was wide-ranging, yet he used what he knew discreetly and with a light touch.

Just as in *The Nature of the Judicial Process*, Cardozo analyzed the process of judging through four different methods, so in his lecture on "Law and Literature," speaking as the master rhetorician, and, as he said, searching the archives of his memory, he discerned six distinct methods of writing: the magisterial or imperative; the laconic or sententious; the conversational or homely; the refined or artificial, "smelling of the lamp, verging at times upon preciosity"; the demonstrative or persuasive type; the agglutinative type that uses the shears and the pastepot. Much of the lecture is then devoted to illustrate and discuss these various types of writing as reflected in legal opinions. On the relation of substance to form in literature, Cardozo quotes a passage from one of the letters of Henry James that makes the point that they are indivisible. "Don't let any one persuade you," James wrote, "... that strenuous selection and comparison are not the very essence of art, and that Form is not substance to that degree that there is absolutely no substance without it. Form alone *takes*. And holds and preserves substance, saves it from the welter of helpless verbiage." The passage from James is followed by Cardozo saying, "This is my own faith."[6] The intertwining of substance and form is an organic process that culminates in the discovery of just the right word or phrase. In *The Growth of the Law* Cardozo described the process: "The search is for the just word, the happy phrase, that will give expression to the thought, but somehow the thought itself is transfigured by the phrase when found. There is emancipation in our very bonds. The restraint of rhyme or metre, the exigencies of period or balance, liberate at times the thought which they confine, and in imprisoning release."[7]

Cardozo's reflections on the practice of judging and of judicial writing clearly, convincingly demonstrate his keen philosophic mind and his mastery of Aristotle's treatises on logic, rhetoric and poetics, no less than those on ethics, politics, and metaphysics. The ancient rabbis said, "The main thing is not learning a lesson but acting upon the lesson one has learned." As many of his judicial opinions show, as we will see, Cardozo applied the lessons he had learned.

II

An opinion of Cardozo's that has become a landmark in tort law is *MacPherson v. Buick Motor Company*, decided in 1916.[8] The opinion illustrates how Cardozo applied the sociological approach in decision making. The plaintiff had purchased a Buick car from an authorized dealer and was injured while driving the car. The injury was caused by a defective spoke of a wheel. The owner of the car had no contractual relationship with the manufacturer, so the company argued that it had no duty to the owner, that it had a contractual relationship only to the dealer. The manufacturer cited precedents that went back to the stagecoach days. Cardozo, writing for the Court of Appeals, upheld the plaintiff's claim. The law had been settled in most jurisdictions that buyers of a product could not sue the manufacturer for negligence if they made the purchase from a dealer and not from the manufacturer. Cardozo, however, argued that the applicable test should be that the manufacturer should be liable for any harm that the product could foreseeably cause. The manufacturer knew that the dealer was not purchasing cars for his own use but for those who would purchase them from him.

Arguing from analogies, Cardozo looked past rules to an underlying principle, which he saw as allowing an injured party to recover from the manufacturer with whom he had had no direct dealing. The manufacturer has duties not only to its dealers but also to the users of its products. "Precedents drawn from the days of travel by stage coach do not fit the conditions of travel today," wrote Cardozo. *MacPherson* in time became the ruling case in almost all jurisdictions. Today consumers universally look to the manufacturer as an implied guarantor of the safety of its product. In July 1998 Ralph Nader, leading proponent of consumer interests, announced his intention to establish a Museum of American Tort Law in his hometown of Winsted, Connecticut. The museum, he said, would exhibit some consumer products that notoriously have been held to have been negligently made— "the Pinto with the exploding gas tank, inflammable pajamas, asbestos, and breast implants..." The museum might well be dedicated to the memory of Judge Benjamin N. Cardozo, as the father of American consumer-protection law.[9]

Another tort case in which Cardozo's opinion for the Court of Appeals has become famous and a favorite of law professors is *Palsgraf v. Long Island Railroad Co.*, decided in 1928.[10] Helen Palsgraf, after buying a ticket, stood on a platform waiting for a train. A train stopped but was going to another destination. A man ran to catch the train that was already moving. He was carrying a package. He jumped aboard a car. He seemed unsteady as if about to fall. A guard on the car, who held the door open, reached forward to help him, and another guard on the platform pushed him from behind. As this was going on, the passenger lost hold of the package and it fell upon the rails. It was a small package, wrapped in newspapers, and one could not tell its contents from its appearance. In fact it contained fireworks, and when it fell it exploded. At the other end of the platform, many feet away, there stood scales, near which stood the plaintiff. The explosion caused the scales to fall upon the plaintiff and injured her. She sued the railroad company, charging negligence.

Some acts, Cardozo wrote, are so imminently dangerous, that one acts at one's peril; for example, if one shoots, one may be liable if the missile strikes a person who was not expected to be where he in fact was standing. In such a case one may speak of negligence as a sort of floating concept. Normally, however, negligence must be spoken of in relation to a defined situation. The passenger who carried the fireworks, an inherently dangerous object, might be liable to the plaintiff, but the railroad had no knowledge of the contents of the package; it is not an insurer against all hazards. The law must define the "orbit of duty"—"the orbit of the danger as disclosed to the eye of reasonable vigilance would be the orbit of the duty." If a person jostles a person standing next to him in a crowd, he does not thereby invade the rights of others standing at the outer fringe of the crowd if the person he jostles happens to carry a bomb—though the man who carried the bomb may be liable. "Life will have to be made over, and human nature transformed, before prevision so extravagant can be accepted as the norm of conduct, the customary standard to which behavior must conform." What the plaintiff in a negligence suit must show is a wrong to herself, a violation of her own right, violation of a duty owed to her, not merely a wrong done to someone else—not just a wrong in general, but specifically a wrong to herself. "The risk reasonably to be perceived defines the duty to be obeyed," and judged by this test, it cannot be said that the railroad company failed in its duty to Helen Palsgraf, for there was nothing in the situation "to suggest to the most cautious mind that the parcel wrapped in newspaper would spread wreckage through the station.... Negligence, like risk, is thus a term of relation. Negligence in the abstract, apart from things related, is surely not a tort, if indeed it is understandable at all."

Palsgraf was the kind of case that gave Cardozo the opportunity to function at his best as a common law judge. It offered him, as he wrote in *The Growth of the Law*, "the same power of creation that built up the common law through its exercise by the judges of the past."[11] In this case, Cardozo was not satisfied simply to examine precedents, he studied them and thought them through to a formulation of the meaning of negligence as a tort. His opinion enriched the literature of the law and contributed to its philosophy. In his biography of Cardozo, Andrew Kaufman noted that the opinion made a big impact in the legal world. "The bizarre facts, ... its adaptability for legal teaching, ... Cardozo's rhetoric, and Cardozo's name—all these factors combined to make *Palsgraf* a legal landmark."[12]

Another tort case, *Wagner v. International Railway Company*,[13] decided in 1921, contributed to Cardozo's fame and manifests the great sensitivity with which he weighed facts. Arthur Wagner and his cousin were on a train together. The cousin fell from the train whose doors had been left open. Wagner got off and walked back four hundred feet along a trestle to look for his cousin. It was night. The cousin was killed, Wagner was injured. He sued the railroad company, alleging that it was negligent in causing the death of his cousin and that his own injuries were the result of the negligence. The jury found for the railroad and the Appellate Division affirmed. The Court of Appeals reversed and sent the case back to the trial court. The new trial was instructed to determine whether the cousin's death was due to the railroad's negligence and whether Wagner was also negligent and thus contributed to his own injury.

On appeal to the Court of Appeals, the company's position was that Wagner's walk along the trestle was his own decision and that it was an intervening cause that broke the causal sequence between any railroad negligence and Wagner's injuries, that the negligence to the cousin was not the proximate cause of injury to Wagner—it was he himself who chose to go out in the dark to search for his cousin.

With three brief words Cardozo wiped out the railroad's claim: "Danger invites rescue." Wagner's reaction was "natural and probable." The "wrong that imperils life is a wrong to the imperilled victim; it is a wrong also to his rescuer." Just as the railroad had violated its duty to the cousin, so, too, had it violated its duty to his rescuer. If the company had not foreseen that there would be an action by a rescuer, it should have foreseen it; for the rescue "is the child of the occasion."

The *Wagner* case is an instance of the deeply sensitive nature of Cardozo's judicial conscience. Wagner in his mind heard his cousin's cry of distress, and he heard it as a summons to him to seek the rescue. "The law," said Cardozo, "does not ignore these reactions of the mind."

If one were to select one aspect of law to which, above all others, Cardozo made his greatest contribution, perhaps it would be the law of torts—civil wrongs, like negligence, for which the injured party may be entitled to compensation. But his influence reached into many other aspects of law, including breach of contract, agency, partnership, equity, corporations, wills, trusts, insurance, and many other substantive as well as procedural aspects.[14]

An opinion by Cardozo relating to the fiduciary duties of persons standing, in relation to each other, in a position akin to partners, *Meinhard v. Salmon*, decided in 1928,[15] has been justly admired and has made its influence felt. Salmon leased from the owner real estate located at the corner of 42nd Street and Fifth Avenue in Manhattan. The lease was to run for twenty years, 1902–1922. Needing the necessary funds for the deal, Salmon entered into a written agreement with Meinhard that was in the nature of a joint venture akin to a partnership. Meinhard advanced half the needed funds for the reconstruction, management and operation of the property, in return for which he was to receive 40 percent of the profits for the first five years and thereafter 50 percent. Salmon was to have sole power to manage and operate the property. At first there were losses, which they shared equally, then there were heavy profits. Less than four months before the end of the twenty-year lease; the owner of the property, who also owned adjoining properties, approached Salmon with a proposal, that ultimately resulted in a lease between a company owned by Salmon and the owner of the total properties comprised of the original property and the properties adjoining it. The lease was for twenty years with an option to extend it to eighty years at the will of Salmon or the owner.

Salmon kept the negotiations secret, so that Meinhard knew nothing about them. Meinhard learned of the transaction only after the new lease was signed. When he learned of the new lease, he demanded that it be held in trust as an asset of the original venture between himself and Salmon and offered to share the obligations. Salmon refused.

The Court of Appeals upheld the claim of Meinhard, and in the court's opinion by Cardozo it said, "Joint adventurers, like copartners, owe to one another, while the enterprise continues, the duty of the finest loyalty.... A trustee is held to something stricter than the morals of the market place. Not honesty alone, but the punctilio of an honor the most sensitive, is then the standard of behavior.... Only thus has the level of conduct for fiduciaries been kept at a higher level than that trodden by the crowd. It will not consciously be lowered by any judgment of this court."

Attorneys for Salmon cited precedents which they interpreted to be favorable to the defendant, but Cardozo brushed them aside: "Little profit will come from a discussion of the precedents. None precisely similar is cited in the briefs of counsel. What is similar in many, or so it seems to us, is the animating principle." What is the principle? It is that a co-adventurer who is also the manager must give his partner "a loyalty that is undivided and unselfish." For a person in the position of Salmon, a managing co-adventurer, "the rule of undivided loyalty is relentless and supreme."[16]

In *Law and Literature*, Cardozo said that clearness is the sovereign quality that an opinion must have, but it is not the only quality that the judge must seek; sometimes the opinion will need to have "the impressive virtue of sincerity and fire."[17] Obviously, *Meinhard v. Salmon* needed this quality; Cardozo wrote his opinion with his conscience and heart as well as with his mind. Judge Richard Posner has pointed out that as of 1990, Cardozo's opinion had been cited no less than 653 times! It was obviously a seminal opinion. His words are memorable "and they set a tone. They make the difference between an arm's length relationship and a fiduciary relationship vivid, unforgettable."[18] In the judgment of Dean Russell Niles, *Meinhard* is "the most important modern decision on fiduciary responsibility," that the opinion of Cardozo changed the code of ethics of fiduciaries from what it had been in the nineteenth century to make it one that was needed in the twentieth century.[19] That was no small achievement.

An equally famous opinion by Cardozo in a contract case was *Wood v. Lucy, Lady Duff-Gordon*, decided in 1917.[20] The defendant was a well-known fashion designer, whose "seal of approval" helped the sale of dresses and other articles. She gave the plaintiff the exclusive right, subject to her approval, to place her endorsement on articles designed by others, and the exclusive right to place her own designs on sale or to license others to market them. In return, the defendant was to receive one-half of all profits from any contracts plaintiff might make. The exclusive rights were to last one year, and thereafter from year to year unless terminated by ninety-day notice. The plaintiff charged that the defendant broke the contract by placing her endorsement on articles without his knowledge and that she kept the profits to herself.

The defendant argued that the arrangement lacked the elements of a contract, for, she argued, the plaintiff bound himself to nothing, he made no promises to do anything. Was there a legally binding contract? It is true, Cardozo held, that the plaintiff made no promise "in so many words" that he will make reasonable efforts to market defendant's designs and endorsements: "we think, however, that such a promise is fairly to be implied. The law has outgrown its primitive stage of formalism when the precise word was the sovereign talisman, and every slip was fatal. It takes a broader view today. A promise may be lacking, and yet the whole writing may be 'instinct with an obligation', imperfectly expressed. If that is so, there is a contract." Cardozo pointed out that the defendant gave *exclusive* rights to the plaintiff: "The acceptance of the exclusive agency was an assumption of its duties." Defendant was to receive one-half of the profits. Unless the plaintiff brought in the business, there would be no profits, no business. The plaintiff promised to give a monthly accounting. The implication is clearly that the plaintiff had duties; that he promised to use reasonable efforts to bring profits into existence; that the monthly accounts would be meaningful.

During the twenty-three years when Cardozo was in private practice, he handled many contract cases and learned much about business practices. He brought his knowledge to bear in the contract cases that were brought to the Court of Appeals, and he asked himself in every instance what it was that the parties wanted to achieve by the bargain they had made between themselves. He knew that the parties sometimes failed to express clearly what was intended; this was obviously the case in *Lady Duff-Gordon*. In all instances, I think, Cardozo held to the ideal of fairness, the principle that the law must be on the side of fair-dealing, that the result will be fair and just, that it will meet the principles of natural justice and the dictates of conscience. To achieve a just decision, he was willing to transcend technicalities and formalities that had become hindrances and obstacles to the fair administration of justice. To achieve this end, Cardozo relied on what he had learned from his experience as a practitioner. "The life of the law," Justice Holmes wrote in *The Common Law*, "has not been logic; it has been experience."

III

Cardozo, already in his early sixties, readily agreed to allow President Herbert Hoover to nominate him as associate justice of the United States Supreme Court, and when the Senate unanimously confirmed the nomination, he moved to Washington. He was not, however, happy to leave the Court of Appeals, where he felt that he was in a friendly company with colleagues who thought, argued, and associated in a spirit of collegiality and mutual friendly and respectful regard. When the Court of Appeals was in session, all the judges lived together in the same hotel in Albany, ate together, spent their leisure time together. When they met in conference, they discussed the cases in a free exchange of views. It was quite different in Washington. Cardozo arrived there when the Supreme Court met in the old quarters, Justices had no offices or chambers in the building but had them in their homes. Apart from their conferences, the Justices saw very little of each other. There was little of the collegiality to which Cardozo had become accustomed. Justice James Clark McReynolds was a special problem, for he was an anti-Semite who would not speak with Justice Brandeis nor with Justice Cardozo. He was nasty, rude, and sarcastic. He was intolerant of female attorneys. When Cardozo delivered an opinion from the bench on opinion day, McReynolds would hold a brief or record in front of his face. When Cardozo died, McReynolds did not attend any of the three memorial sessions held at the Supreme Court.[21]

During his first year in Washington, there were moments when Cardozo felt wretched, disconsolate, and said to his caring friend and housekeeper, Kate Tracy, that he wished he were dead.[22] Being a justice of the Supreme Court was an honor that Cardozo welcomed, but it was one for which he paid a high price. He was now only one-ninth of the court on which he sat.[23] In a letter to Felix Frankfurter, in 1932, he wrote: "I don't believe that I'll ever have the influence here that I have had at Albany."[24]

Cardozo joined the Supreme Court at a time when the country was in a deep depression, and when the Court, unfortunately, was dominated by an entrenched conservative majority that stood in the way of New Deal legislation. Cardozo, Brandeis, and Harlan F. Stone , who were sometimes joined by Chief Justice Charles Evans Hughes, were the dissenting liberals. In desperation, President Franklin D. Roosevelt, in February 1937, sent to Congress a bill that proposed legislation that came to be called the Court-Packing Plan. If enacted, it would have allowed the president to nominate additional justices so that a majority would uphold the constitutionality of his New Deal legislation. The bill was widely denounced by Republicans and even by moderate Democrats. In March, however, a radical change took place in the Court as Justice Owen Roberts, who held the swing vote, moved over to join the liberal justices, and the court now, by 5–4 vote, upheld the constitutionality of a state minimum wage law and the National Labor Relations Act. This was the "switch in time that saved nine."[25] Later in the same year, Justice Willis Van Devanter resigned and was replaced by Hugo L. Black, so that there was a solid liberal majority even without Justice Roberts.

It was in this setting that Cardozo was assigned to write the majority opinions in two important New Deal cases. In *Steward Machine Co. v. Davis*, decided in 1937,[26] by a 5–4 vote, the Court upheld a part of the Social Security Act of 1935 that set up mechanisms for unemployment compensation. Cardozo wrote that the payroll tax on employers that produced the revenue to fund unemployment compensation was constitutional under the provision of the Constitution that grants power to Congress to tax to provide for the general welfare of the United States, and that the Tenth Amendment was not a restriction on the taxing and spending power of Congress. In a companion case, decided at the same time, *Helvering v. Davis*,[27] with only Justices Butler and McReynolds dissenting, the Court upheld the constitutionality of the old-age benefits provision of the Social Security Act. Writing for the majority, Cardozo said that the act was passed in response to a nationwide calamity that could not be solved without federal action. If the problem were left to the states, some would fund programs and some would not, and industries would leave the states that funded programs and indigents would flock to these states. Federal action was imperative, and the Tenth Amendment was held not to stand in the way.

In these cases Cardozo used the sociological approach that he wrote about in his famous book, *The Nature of the Judicial Process*. His opinions in these cases have stood the test of time as formulations of the power of the federal government to act for the "general welfare" by use of the power of Congress to tax and to spend.

Cardozo's more significant and more influential opinion was, however, in *Palko v. Connecticut*, decided in 1937,[28] about one-half year before his death. It is not unusual for a state to try a defendant twice for the same crime, as when a conviction is set aside on account of some error at the trial that was prejudicial to the defendant. *Palko*, however, was different, for the defendant was convicted for second-degree murder and sentenced for life, but the state, not the defendant, appealed. It argued that the defendant had been indicted for first-, not second-, degree murder, and the trial court had committed errors that were prejudicial to the state, that they were such as prevented the state from getting a conviction for first-degree murder. The Connecticut Supreme Court of Errors set aside the conviction and ordered a new trial, at which the defendant was found guilty of first-degree murder, and he was sentenced to death. The case was an unusual one. In his appeal to the United States Supreme Court, Palko argued that the second trial had put him in jeopardy twice, within the meaning of the Fifth Amendment, and that the Due Process Clause of the Fourteenth Amendment had, by implication, adopted the double jeopardy prohibition.

On appeal to the United States Supreme Court, the defendant's conviction for first-degree murder was upheld. In his opinion for eight of the justices (only Justice Butler dissented), Cardozo wrote that the protection against double jeopardy was not "fundamental" and was, therefore, not an element in the guarantee of due process. He explained why some rights were of a higher order than others and, therefore, became binding on the states.

In 1833 Chief Justice John Marshall wrote for a unanimous Supreme Court that the Bill of Rights was binding only on the federal government, not on the states.[29] The defendant in *Palko*, however, argued that whatever would be a violation of the Bill of Rights if done by the federal government, is equally unlawful if done by a state, by force of the Fourteenth Amendment guarantee that no person shall be deprived, by any act of the state, of his life, liberty, or property without due process of law. "There is no such general rule," wrote Cardozo. The Due Process Clause, he said, does make it unlawful for a state to abridge the freedom of speech that is guaranteed by the First Amendment, or freedom of the press, or the free exercise of religion, or the right of peaceable assembly, or the right of a person accused of crime to the benefit of counsel. These rights are valid against the federal government by reason of specific guarantees in the Bill of Rights, and they also have been found "to be implicit in the concept of ordered liberty, and thus, through the Fourteenth Amendment, become valid as against the states."

By what "rationalizing principle" is the selection made so that some rights are found to be "implicit in the concept of ordered liberty" and some not? The rights that have been upheld against the states have achieved this result, not because they were automatically or mechanically transferred from the Bill of Rights to the Fourteenth Amendment, but rather, they were absorbed into the Due Process Clause only because, after careful study, they were found to be "fundamental" to our notions of liberty and justice, only because "they represented the very essence of a scheme of ordered liberty, ... principles of justice so rooted in the traditions and conscience of our people as to be ranked fundamental."

This case marked the beginning or became the forerunner of the most significant constitutional debate of the twentieth century, and the opinion of Cardozo has played a key role in the debate.

Ten years after *Palko*, the debate reached its most intense stage in *Adamson v. California*.[30] The Fifth Amendment bans compelling a defendant to incriminate himself in any federal trial. But does this guarantee apply as well to a trial in a state court? The majority of justices in this case adopted the approach of Cardozo as formulated in *Palko* and held that the Fourteenth Amendment "does not draw all the rights of the federal Bill of Rights under its protection" but incorporates only those that are so fundamental that they are "implicit in the concept of ordered liberty." It held that the state is not bound to observe the prohibition against self-incrimination.

Justices Black and Douglas (with whom Justices Murphy and Rutledge substantially agreed) read the Fourteenth Amendment as a guarantee that no state may deprive a person of any right enumerated in the Bill of Rights. According to this opinion, all the provisions of the Bill of Rights have been "incorporated" into the Due Process Clause of the Fourteenth Amendment. Justice Black contended that the history of the adoption of the Fourteenth Amendment shows that this result was the intention of the framers and all who were responsible for its enactment. He attacked Cardozo's approach in *Palko*: "I further contend that the 'natural law' formula which the Court uses ... should be abandoned as an incongruous excrescence on our Constitution."

Justice Frankfurter, who was a member of the Court's majority, had a slightly different approach. He wrote that when a conviction in a state court is before the Court for review under a claim that a right protected by the Due Process Clause of the Fourteenth Amendment has been denied, the issue is not whether a provision of the federal Bill of Rights has been violated, The question is whether the proceedings at the trial offended "those canons of decency and fairness which express the notions of justice of English-speaking peoples." This came to be known as the "fairness" test. It is not, in essence, different from Cardozo's test as formulated in *Palko*.

Black believed in absolutes. He wanted the Constitution as written to serve as a complete guide to decisions in constitutional cases. He was opposed to the idea that some rights or immunities are fundamental, while others are of lesser rank, less importance.

The Court has not followed Justice Black's proposal, it has not read into the Due Process Clause all of the first eight amendments that are in the Bill of Rights, but has proceeded on a case-by-case process. In doing so, it implicitly shares the method of the common law to which Cardozo was deeply devoted from the days when he was in private practice. He wanted principles to evolve out of facts. The Court, moving on a case-by-case basis, has "incorporated" most of the guarantees of the Bill of Rights. Black's approach has now only a historical interest, while Cardozo's has won a fixed important place in constitutional adjudication.

Cardozo's concept of fundamental rights is also very important because it makes possible the recognition of rights that are not spelled out in the Bill of Rights. It makes possible the recognition of an unwritten Bill of Rights, one that includes, for example, the right of privacy, the right to an abortion. Justice Black dissented in *Griswold v. Connecticut*,[31] in which the Court upheld the right of privacy, although recognizing that it is not explicitly enumerated in the Bill of Rights. Black's approach would require an amendment to the Constitution.

Another very significant result of Cardozo's idea that some rights are fundamental: If the right is fundamental, then any governmental action that impinges on it is subjected to "strict scrutiny"—the government must show that its action is closely related to a compelling governmental interest. In other cases, the government needs to show only that its action relates to a legitimate governmental interest. In other words, it might be said that when strict scrutiny is required, the government must try to overcome a presumption of unconstitutionality, while in other cases, the government's action is presumed to be constitutional and the burden of proof of unconstitutionality is on the party challenging the government's action. The result of this differentiation or hierarchy of rights has been that there are very few cases in which governmental action infringing on a fundamental right has succeeded in passing the strict scrutiny test. The federal government is limited in its powers and actions by the guarantees of the Bill of Rights, and the states are limited in their powers and actions by the *fundamental rights, liberties, immunities, and privileges* that are guaranteed by the provision in the Fourteenth Amendment that no person may be deprived of his life, liberty or property without due process of law. Cardozo's contribution to this development of American constitutional law is very great. It is a substantial part of his monumental legacy.

IV

In his lifetime Cardozo was justly lionized by lawyers, judges, professors of law, indeed by whoever knew him or knew about him. Acquaintances and friends remarked about his natural courtesy and kindness, his integrity, honesty and serenity. Judge Learned Hand said that by common consent of the bench and bar of the State of New York, Cardozo had no equal, that he was a person who, "by the gentleness and purity of his character, the acuteness and suppleness of his mind, by his learning, his moderation, and his sympathetic understanding of his time, has won an unrivaled esteem wherever else [beyond the State of New York] he is known."[32] This estimate of Cardozo's character was written by Judge Hand in 1922. Seventy or eighty years later it can safely be repeated as a just characterization. No other jurist, perhaps no other American in public life, has achieved equal esteem, reverential regard.

Many have written or spoken of Cardozo's "saintly" character. The author of the most comprehensive biography of Cardozo, Professor Andrew L. Kaufman, questions the propriety of the use of this adjective. Cardozo was, he says, "a human being and not a bloodless, idealized essence." He was, says Kaufman, proud and vain, "he had saintly manner and was saintly toward Nellie (his older sister with whom be lived), but he was no saint." However, the only evidence I could find of Cardozo's alleged pride and vanity is the satisfaction and happiness he derived from being a well-born Sephardic Jew whose ancestors were settled in America before the Revolution and were famous rabbis, scholars, and community leaders—among his relatives were the Nathans, the Seixas family, Emma Lazarus. He would have been a boor not to have felt deep satisfaction in having these distinguished relationships. To call such a natural feeling by terms that could be read as pejorative is to misjudge the person. And when men who were themselves eminent judges, lawyers, and community leaders spoke of Cardozo as a saint, they meant, not that he lived on locusts and wild honey, but that he was a man of great virtue and benevolence; they meant that as Learned Hand said, "the purity and elevation of his character set him in a class apart."[33]

His close friend Irving Lehman, chief judge of the New York Court of Appeals after Cardozo left for Washington, remembered Cardozo, not as a proud and vain man, but one who was "shy and retiring":

> Many have found his mental ability remarkable. His friends know that the beauty of his character, his selfless devotion to his work, his firm adherence to principle and ... his love for his friends and his perfect charity to all men were far more remarkable....
>
> In his heart there was love so great that it excluded all other feelings. Shy and retiring though he was, he found his greatest happiness ... in the companionship of his friends. The great legal thinker was at all times and under all circumstances the gentle, modest, loving man.[34]

Professor Milton Handler has written that once when Cardozo was a guest for dinner at his home, Mrs. Handler, in the course of a conversation, remarked that she had written a master's dissertation on colonial literature, and Cardozo showed that he was fully familiar with the writings of John Cotton, Thomas Hooker, Cotton Mather, and other "builders of the Bay Colony." Cardozo appeared to be fully familiar with that recondite field "as indeed he was with all phases of English and American literature, to say nothing about his prodigious learning in philosophy and related fields."[35]

V

Cardozo took great satisfaction in being a member of the Spanish-Portuguese Congregation Shearith Israel, that built its first synagogue in 1730. Cardozo was a fourth generation member. His bar-mitzvah was celebrated in the congregation's synagogue. Soon after his bar-mitzvah, Cardozo stopped attending services and observing the ceremonial laws; but he and Nellie kept pork products and shellfish out of their home. When some members of the congregation agitated to end the separation of the sexes at services, Cardozo attended a meeting and spoke eloquently against the change, and the congregation remained strictly Orthodox. The late Professor Harry A. Wolfson, when asked how he identified himself religiously, replied that he was a "non-observant Orthodox Jew." If pressed, perhaps Cardozo, too, would thus identify himself, and do so smilingly.

Influenced by Louis Brandeis, Rabbi Stephen Wise, and Judge Julian Mack, Cardozo joined the Zionist organization. He also was a member of the American Jewish Committee and held important positions in the organization. He served on the board of governors of the Hebrew University in Jerusalem, and was a member of the executive committee of the Jewish Welfare Board. As a member of the board of trustees of Columbia University, he served on the committee that met with the advisor to Jewish students. Some of his closest friends were leading American Jews, including Rabbi Stephen Wise, Louis Marshall, Justice Brandeis, Justice Felix Frankfurter, Abram Elkus, and Irving Lehman. In his will, he left a bequest to assure perpetual care of the family's plot in the cemetery of Shearith Israel, where he was to be interred, and a sum to endow a bed at Mount Sinai Hospital in memory of his sister Emily, and $25,000 (in 1990s' dollars, $325,000) to the federated Jewish charities society of New York.

In 1931, in a talk at the Institute of Jewish Religion, of which Stephen Wise was the head, Cardozo told his audience what religion (including, of course, Judaism) meant to him:

> The submergence of self in the pursuit of an ideal, the readiness to spend oneself without measure, prodigally, almost ecstatically, for something intuitively apprehended as great and noble, spend one self one knows not why—some of us like to believe that is what religion means.[36]

In an address delivered at a dinner honoring the rabbi of his congregation, Cardozo, commenting on Pascal's belief in God, gave his own view of Judaism:

> Pascal's outlook on life was essentially Hebraic. He made conduct, in [Matthew] Arnold's phrase, four-fifths of life.... Indeed, if I had to choose, I should have to say that there is matter for religion in any and every activity that has relation to the good life in all its fullness and perfection.

And he quoted the prophet Micah that the Lord requires only that we do justice, love mercy, and walk humbly with God.[37]

I have no doubt that Cardozo believed that he was trying as a jurist to fulfill God's command to act as God's surrogate in administering justice—that this was his station and that this was his station's duty. To fulfill his calling as a jurist, he had to be a lawyer, a philosopher, a moralist, a sociologist, a historian, a rhetorician—"if one is the mouthpiece of divinity."[38]

Notes

1. Kaufman, Andrew L., *Cardozo* (1998) p. 119. Hereafter this work will be referred to as Kaufman. This is by far the most comprehensive and best biography of Cardozo.
2. Ibid., 196.
3. Ibid., 132.
4. Richard A., *Law and Literature* (1988), 293
5. Kaufman, 157.
6. Cardozo, *Law and Literature and Other Essays and Addresses* (1931), p. 5.
7. Cardozo, *The Growth of the Law* (1924).
8. *MacPherson v. Buick Co.*, 217 N.Y. 382 (1916).
9. *New York Times*, July 28, 1998, p. 1.
10. *Palsgraf v. Long Is. Railroad Co.*, 248 N. Y. 339 (1928).
11. *The Growth of the Law*, 137.
12. Kaufman, 303.
13. *Wagner v. Intern. Railway Co.*,232 N.Y. 176 (1921).
14. See Levy, Beryl H., *Cardozo and Frontiers of Legal Thinking* (1938, 1969) for selected cases on various topics.
15. *Meinhard v. Salmon*, 249 N.Y. 458 (1928).
16. Ibid., 464.
17. *Law and Literature*, 9.
18. Posner, op. cit. supra note 4, at pp. 104–5.
19. Kaufman, 241.
20. *Woody v. Lucy, Lady Duff-Gordon*, 222 N.Y. 88 (1917).
21. Kaufman, 480.
22. Ibid., 475.
23. Milton Handler and Michael Ruby, "Justice Cardozo, One-Ninth of the Supreme Court," *Cardozo Law Rev* 10:1–2, Oct.-Nov.1988.
24. Kaufman, 480.
25. *West Coast Hotel Co. v Parrish*, 300 U. S. 379 (1937); *NLRB v. Jones & Laughlin Steel Corp.*, 301 U. S. 1 (1937).
26. *Steward Machine Co. v. Davis*, 301 U. S. 548 (1937).
27. *Helvering v. Davis*, 301 U. S. 619 (1937).
28. *Palko v. Connecticut*, 302 U. S. 319 (1937); overruled in *Benton v. Maryland*, 395 U.S. 784 (1969).
29. *Barron v. Baltimore*, 32 U. S. 243 (1833).
30. *Adamson v. California* 332 U. S. v. 46 (1947), overruled in *Griffin v. California*, 380 U. S. 609 (1965).

31. *Griswold v. Connecticut*, 381 U. S. 479 (1965).
32. Kaufman, 219.
33. Ibid.,112, 153, 161, 183, 419.
34. Handler and Ruby, "Justice Cardozo," supra at 244.
35. Idem.
36. Kaufman, 190.
37. Ibid., 189.
38. Cardozo, *Law and Literature*, 14.

6

Felix Frankfurter

Felix Frankfurter (1882-1965) came to America as an immigrant at the age of twelve, when he spoke no English but spoke Yiddish and knew Hebrew. He came from an Orthodox Jewish family in Vienna; his father had studied to be a rabbi. In his mature years he described himself as being a "believing unbeliever." Like his friend Morris Raphael Cohen, he attended City College of New York, and then at Harvard Law School, from which he graduated first in his class.

Frankfurter, as a young man, joined Louis D. Brandeis in work on Zionism. In 1921 he went to Paris with the Zionist delegation to the Peace Conference at the end of World War I. He met Emir Feisal, head of the Arab delegation, and following their talk Feisal sent Frankfurter the historic letter, dated February 3, 1919, that stated that the Arab delegation regarded the Zionist proposal as "moderate and proper," that Jews would be welcome to their "home," and that the Zionist and Arab movements complement and need one another. In 1921, when Brandeis withdrew from leadership of the Zionist movement, Frankfurter also withdrew, but continued his interest in the building of a national Jewish home in Palestine and publicly attacked the government of Great Britain for its misuse and perversion of its mandatory responsibilities in Palestine.

Before be died he left instruction that a Jewish prayer be recited at his funeral. He said that Professor Louis Henkin, his former clerk, would know what prayer be meant. It was, of course, the Kaddish. He explained that he was born a Jew and wished to die as a Jew.

In the article on Frankfurter in the authoritative *Oxford Companion to the Supreme Court of the United States* (1992), Professor Peter Charles Hoffer wrote,

> The rabbinical scholarship of the Talmud speaks of obligations, not of rights. The Jew is commanded to do justice, love mercy, and walk humbly with God. The way to understand these and the many other *mitzot* (God's laws) is study, study of law. Frankfurter's belief in duty, the duty of one individual to another, of the government to individuals, of individuals to government, is all of a piece with Jewish law. Justice Frankfurter's Process jurisprudence is a philosophy of obligations....

> If one concedes that this rabbinical fidelity to law lay deep in Frankfurter's consciousness, his life and career no longer appear marked by contradiction. Throughout his life, he honored the obligation to teach, to study, and to live by law, and he exalted this principle on the eve of his passing [by requesting that Kaddisb be recited at his death].

Justice Frankfurter's philosophy of obligation, though never explicitly formulated by him, was perhaps rooted in classical Jewish thought. I shall test this hypothetical philosophy in an analysis of Frankfurter's opinions in the *Flag Salute Cases* and the *Sunday Closing Laws Cases*, cases that implicated his experience as a Jew and as an American. An essay by me on Frankfurter as a masterful legal historian was published in *Essays in Legal History in Honor of Felix Frankfurter,* edited by Morris D. Forkoscb (1966).

*   *   *

When Felix Frankfurter was appointed associate justice of the Supreme Court of the United States by President Franklin D. Roosevelt in 1939, it was generally assumed that be would become one of America's greatest jurists. Cardozo had been appointed to fill the chair vacated by Holmes, and Frankfurter wag appointed to fill the chair vacated by Cardozo, and it was thought that be would become a fourth member of the pantheon comprised of Holmes, Brandeis and Cardozo. This has not happened.

It was also generally thought that Frankfurter would be a great liberal justice, a jurist whose constitutionalism would be associated with that of Holmes, Brandeis and Cardozo. When one thinks of the important liberal justices, one thinks of these justices and of Harlan F. Stone, Hugo L. Black, William 0. Douglas, Wiley B. Rutledge, Frank Murphy, Earl Warren, William J. Brennan, Arthur J. Goldberg (who succeeded Frankfurter), Abe Fortas, and Thurgood Marshall. But the name of Felix Frankfurter has no place among them. There was very good reason for the expectation that Frankfurter would be strongly liberal. Everything in his background pointed in that direction: he was a close friend of Holmes and Brandeis; a friend of Cardozo; a friend and adviser of President Roosevelt; he was instrumental in saving Thomas L. Mooney from execution; he wrote a book in defense of Sacco and Vanzetti; he was foremost authority on administrative law (an essential element of the New Deal); be was closely identified with the liberal journal, *The Nation*, and with the American Civil Liberties Union.

Frankfurter is not the only justice who disappointed expectations. Earl Warren, when be was attorney general of California, demanded the evacuation of the Japanese from the West Coast during World War II. He ran as the vice-presidential candidate with Thomas Dewey in 1948. President Eisenhower thought that Warren would be a strong advocate of judicial restraint in the Supreme Court and was grievously disappointed. Eisenhower also deeply regretted his appointment of Brennan as Associate Justice. Both Warren and Brennan were leading activist justices in the promotion of individual rights and liberties and equality, even as Frankfurter became known as a leading advocate of judicial restraint.

I

Frankfurter served as a justice of the Supreme Court for twenty-tree years (1939-62) and wrote hundreds of opinions, yet, unfortunately for his reputation, he is best and most often remembered for his role and opinions in the Flag Salute Cases. It was in one of these cases that he identified himself as a Jew. He wrote: "One who belongs to the most vilified and persecuted minority in history is not likely to be insensible to the freedoms guaranteed by our Constitution." This is perhaps the only instance in the history of the Supreme Court where a justice identified himself, in his opinion, by his religion. His clerks pleaded with Frankfurter to omit this sentence, and a colleague on the bench also tried to dissuade him, but he rebuffed them by saying: "This is my opinion, not yours."

In the first *Flag Salute Case* (*Minersville School District v. Gobitis*[1] decided in 1940, the Court held that a Jehovah's Witness child could constitutionally be expelled from a public school for refusing to participate in saluting the flag and pledging allegiance. The opinion for the Court was by Justice Frankfurter. Justice Stone was the only dissenter.

The case involved two children, aged twelve and ten. The Board of Education of Minersville, Pennsylvania required all pupils and teachers to participate in the ceremony by saluting the flag with the right hand while the pledge of allegiance is spoken in unison. The Gobitis family conscientiously believed that the Bible prohibited participation in the ceremony.

Justice Frankfurter, in his opinion, said that the school board had not adopted the requirement as one aimed to deny any religious liberty to any children; it was intended to be a general regulation aimed to strengthen national unity; for the flag is a symbol of national strength, national unity. Religious, conscientious scruples do not relieve a person from obedience to a general law. "The mere possession of religious convictions which contradict the relevant concerns of a political society does not relieve the citizen from the discharge of political responsibilities." This was the general principle, formulated by Frankfurter, under which the case was to be decided. Looking at the case in its specificity, Frankfurter wrote: "We are dealing with an interest inferior to none in the hierarchy of legal values. National unity is the basis of national security." And the flag salute ceremony in the public schools is intended to foster national unity; it thus represents the highest value. The school board was not required to exempt the Gobitis children from participation, because, said Frankfurter, "such an exemption might introduce elements of difficulty into the school discipline, might cast doubts in the minds of the other children which would themselves weaken the effect of the exercise." Was there no remedy for the Gobites children? Yes, said Frankfurter: in a democracy, individuals may educate the public and the legislature to change the law; the courts are not the only guardians of our liberties.

Justice Stone (later chief justice), lone dissenter, stated that the school board 's regulation coerced the Gobitis children to express a sentiment which they did not entertain and which violated their deepest religious convictions—compulsion that is a prohibited infringement of personal liberty, freedom of speech, freedom of religion, all guaranteed by the Bill of Rights. Government has no right to compel public affirmations that violate the religious conscience. There are other ways, said Stone, to teach loyalty and patriotism than by compelling pupils to affirm that which they do not believe and which violates their religious convictions. The very essence of the liberty guaranteed by the Constitution is "the freedom of the individual from compulsion as to what he shall think and what he shall say, at least where the compulsion is to bear false witness to his religion." Infringements of personal liberty, Stone wrote, have generally been justified by the government, "in the name of righteousness and the public good" and have been generally directed, as in this case, at "politically helpless minorities." Small, discrete, insular minorities need to be protected by subjecting the laws that curtail their liberty to "careful scrutiny."

Stone's and Frankfurter's opinions, when made public, were subjected to the careful scrutiny that had not been given to the school board's action. Legal scholars attacked the Court's decision for failure to give sufficient weight to the guarantees of the Bill of Rights. The Court's decision and the strong language of Frankfurter's opinion justifying the flag salute and the Pledge of Allegiance had the unfortunate effect of provoking mobs to physically attack Jehovah's Witnesses. Jehovah's Witness school children were threatened to be sent to reformatories for juvenile delinquents. Trying to mitigate the situation, Congress in 1942 passed an act making flag observance voluntary; the act however, was effective only on the federal level, but school boards are agencies of the states.

Three years after the *Gobitis* case, the Supreme Court was given an opportunity to reconsider its decision. In the second *Flag Salute Case* (*West Virginia State Board of Education v. Barnette*,[2] 1943). The Supreme Court, by a 6-3 vote, overruled its earlier decision. The Court's opinion by Justice Robert Jackson essentially followed the lead of Stone's dissenting opinion in *Gobitis*, except that he placed emphasis on the fact that saluting the flag is symbolic speech and is, therefore, subject to the guarantee of free speech. This constitutional right of free speech protects silence as well as utterance.

It was the right not to speak for which Thomas More died as a martyr. By a few words he could have saved his life, but his conscience tied his tongue.

Justice Jackson's concluding words have been frequently quoted: "If there is any fixed star in our constitutional constellation, it is that no official, high or petty, can prescribe what shall be orthodox in politics, nationalism, religion, or other matters of opinion or force citizens to confess by word or act their faith therein..."

By making the Free Speech Clause of the First Amendment the foundation of its decision, rather than the Free Exercise Clause, the

Court in this case broadened the reach of its holding. The freedom not to be coerced to avow a belief or an opinion that one does not have is enjoyed by secularists no less than by religious persons, by atheists no less than by, say, Jehovah's Witnesses. Are there constitutional exemptions recognized exclusively for religious believers? We will reserve our answer to this important question for consideration at a later point in our discussion. We return now to Justice Frankfurter's dissenting opinion, that is the main focus of our concern.

II

Justice Frankfurter now, only three years after *Gobitis,* found himself in the uncomfortable position of justifying his earlier opinion against the powerful arguments of Justice Stone's dissenting opinion in *Gobitis* and Justice Jackson's majority opinion in *Barnette.* In his opening paragraph Frankfurter wrote:

> One who belongs to the most vilified and most persecuted minority in history is not likely to be insensible to the freedoms guaranteed by our Constitution. But as judges we are neither Jew nor Gentile, neither Catholic nor agnostic. As a member of this Court I am not justified in writing my private notions of policy into the Constitution, no matter bow deeply I may cherish them or how mischievous I may deem their disregard.

The implication may be that Frankfurter believed that Jackson had written his "private notions of policy into the Constitution." For well over a half century it is the second, and not the first, *Flag Salute Case, Barnette,* and not *Gobitis,* that has stood as the unquestioned constitutional authority. It is still true, as it was in 1943, that, "if there is any fixed star in our constitutional constellation, it is that no official can prescribe what shall be orthodox in politics, nationalism, religion, or force citizens to confess ...their faith therein."

Justice Frankfurter in his dissenting opinion did not address Justice Jackson's opinion. He ignored the opinion and addressed only the decision. He persisted to consider the case as one involving the Free Exercise Clause, not the Free Speech Clause. His intention was only to justify the Court's decision in *Gobitis,* which the Court was now overruling, and to justify his opinion in *Gobitis,* which the Court now was brushing aside as irrelevant. It was all a case of intellectual shadowboxing, each side striking at an opponent who was not really there.

Frankfurter made the following arguments.

1. The rights protected by the Constitution are all equally protected. They are not in a hierarchical arrangement. The right to property is not in any way inferior to the right to religious liberty or free speech.
2. When a state (or one of its subdivisions, e.g., a school board) enacts a law, the Supreme Court should consider it presumptively constitutional, and may set it aside as unconstitutional only if no reasonable mind could justify its enactment. If a law can be said to be "reasonable," or not unreasonable, then it must be upheld as constitutional. And this is so whether the law impinges upon a property right or upon a civil liberty.
3. If a law is enacted with the specific intent to restrict a religious liberty, to restrict or promote a religious creed or community, it should be held to be unconstitutional. However, if a general, non-discriminatory regulation in fact touches an individual's or group's conscientious religious scruples, it is nonetheless enforced as a constitutional exercise of the legislative power.
4. It might be wise for the legislature to provide an exemption from such a law for those whose religious scruples are affected, but the Court has no power to write into the law such exemptions. A court can only strike down, it cannot modify, and it cannot make exemptions from a general requirement. "The constitutional protection of religious freedom terminated disabilities, it did not create new privileges. It gave religious equality, not civil immunity. Its essence is freedom from conformity to religious dogma, not freedom from conformity to law because of religious dogma."
5. As to a law compelling the flag salute and the recital of the Pledge of Allegiance: "an act promoting good citizenship and national allegiance is within the domain of governmental authority," and is constitutional. It is a secular law; its validity cannot be questioned.
6. Parents have a right to choose what school their children should attend. The state has no power to bring private schools under its strict control concerning all details of such schools.
7. If a law is unwise, the remedy should be found through education, public opinion. Illiberal laws cannot be invalidated through court action. "Our constant pre-occupation with the constitutionality of legislation rather than with its wisdom tends to preoccupation of the American mind with a false value."

It is unnerving, deeply distressing to see how a great, first-rate, superior mind could go off on a line of thought that was not only wrong but also perverse and false to his own fundamental convictions. In the annals of constitutional jurisprudence, the dissenting opinion of Justice Frankfurter in the *Second Flag Salute Case* must be considered one of the most erratic, one of the biggest failures, one of the most misguided opinions. His opening statement that as judges "we are neither Jew nor Gentile, neither Catholic nor agnostic," is, of course, the statement of a truism. No one should have expected Frankfurter to see the compulsory flag salute, when challenged by Jehovah's Witness children, from the standpoint of the Jew, or from any narrow parochial, sectarian viewpoint. But Justice Jackson saw that the Founders of the Constitution as they drafted and adopted the First Amendment, with its guarantees of religious liberty and free speech, had in mind the history of religious persecution and the history of political persecution. He knew that the Founders of the Constitution wanted to be sure that the Constitution would protect a person's right to be different, that neither Jew nor gentile, neither Catholic nor atheist, neither Quaker nor Mennonite nor Mormon would be compelled by law to avow beliefs he does not have, be compelled to express opinions he does not believe. I find it impossible to understand how Frankfurter could have misled his mind and heart to approve persecution of the Gobitis children and their parents for refusing to engage in a ceremony tbat they fervently believed to be a form of idol worship. A Justice of the Supreme Court did not need to be a Jew, he only needed to know Andrew D. White's *History of the Warfare of Science with Theology in Christendom* (1896), and Lord Acton's essays on the history of freedom in antiquity and in Christianity (1907), which Frankfurter surely knew, to conclude that the Gobitis children were protected by the Bill of Rights.

Frankfurter's law clerks and his colleague were fully justified when they tried to persuade him not to refer to his being a Jew. It was irrelevant. The bloody history of religious and political persecution should have convinced him, as it did Justice Jackson and a majority of the justices, Jew and gentile alike, that Americans enjoy the constitutional right to differ, and to differ over trivial things and also over "things that touch the heart of the existing order."

III

Frankfurter was not long on the bench when it became clear that be would not be guided by the constitutional doctrines that had been formulated by his predecessors Holmes, Brandeis, and Cardozo, with whom be had close friendship ties. In his *Barnette* dissenting opinion, as we have noted, Frankfurter argued that there is no hierarchy among the rights and liberties protected by the Constitution, that property rights, religious liberty, and freedom of speech are all equally guaranteed, and that a legislative act affecting any right or liberty is to be presumed to be constitutional, and that anyone who challenges the statute has the burden of proving that the act cannot pass the test of being reasonable. Thus, for example, it is not unreasonable for a school board to want to foster patriotism and to advance American nationalism, and to require the flag salute and recitation of the Pledge of Allegiance as means to this end.

All this was contrary to the teaching of Justices Holmes, Brandeis, and Cardozo. In the infamous *Lochner* case (1903) Justice Holmes's dissenting, argued that a state law should be upheld as constitutional unless it is proved that a rational person would be compelled to maintain that it infringes upon a fundamental principle of law and American tradition.[3] In *Abrams v. United States,* [4] Holmes, joined in his dissent by Brandeis, maintained that the rationality test is inapplicable to a law that infringes free press or free speech, for a curtailment of such basic liberties can be upheld only upon a showing of the existence of a "clear and present danger."

Holmes wrote that the First Amendment protected the expression of all opinions "unless they so imminently threaten immediate interference with the lawful and pressing purposes of the law that an immediate check is required to save the country." Thus, economic legislation, such as was before the Court in *Lochner*, needed simply a rational reason to establish its constitutionality, but limitations on a First Amendment freedom faced a much more rigorous test.

This differentiation between the guarantee of property or economic rights, on the one band, and fundamental liberties guaranteed by the Bill of Rights, came to be sharply articulated by Justice Cardozo. In *Palko v. Connecticut* [5] he spelled out what sometimes came to be called the preferred freedoms doctrine, which is that there is a constitutional preference for those "fundamental principles of liberty and justice which lie at the base of all our civil and political institutions." These fundamental principles, said Cardozo, are the matrix, the indispensable condition, of nearly every other form of freedom. Then in a famous Footnote Four in his opinion in *United States v. Carolene Products,*[6] Justice Stone stated that legislation restricting the political process or that is hostile to "discrete and insular minorities" must be subjected to "more exacting judicial scrutiny," that is, more exacting than the mere rationality test.

All these contributions to constitutional doctrine, that came to be firmly accepted by the Court, however, were brushed aside by Frankfurter, who persisted to maintain that there is no hierarchy among American freedoms and liberties, that no liberty is entitled to the test of "strict scrutiny". In *Kovacs v. Cooper* (1949)[7] Frankfurter stated that the ranking of constitutional rights was nothing short of being "mischievous." Yet the ranking has survived Frankfurter's wrongheaded attacks. And strict scrutiny continues to be the standard test in any case that involves the infringement of a fundamental right.

IV

Justice Frankfurter contended that constitutional protection of religious liberty was intended to end disabilities on account of religion but that it did not create new privileges. The Constitution does not create immunity from a general law on account of religion. The First Amendment guarantee of religious freedom creates no exemption from compulsory flag salute for children belonging to the Jehovah's Witness religion.

Twenty-one years after the Court decided the *Second Flag Salute Case*, Justice Frankfurter had another opportunity to consider this question of an exemption from a general law on account of religious belief and observance, and this time the Court had before it not Jehovah's Witnesses but Orthodox Jews.

The time was 1961, when communities throughout the country had laws that required commercial establishments to be closed on Sundays. By the 1980s many such laws bad been repealed, and by the end of the century one hardly ever read or heard about Sunday Closing Laws. In 1961, however, the Supreme Court had to consider four hotly contested cases that involved such laws. One of the cases involved a kosher supermarket that contested the constitutionality of the Massachusetts Sunday Closing Laws, and another that involved merchants in Philadelphia who operated a retail clothing and home furnishings store. We shall confine our discussion to the latter, *Braunfeld v. Brown.*[8]

The plaintiffs, Orthodox Jews, closed their store on Fridays before sunset and kept it closed until nightfall on Saturdays. They previously had kept their store open on Sundays. They sought an injunction against the enforcement of the Pennsylvania Sunday Closing Law, arguing that closing their store on Sundays will render them unable to continue in their business, that enforcement of the law against them will prohibit the free exercise of their religion; that the statute compels them to give up their observance of the Jewish Sabbath, which is a basic tenet of their Orthodox Jewish faith, or, if they observe their Sabbath and keep their store closed also on Sundays, they will be at a serious disadvantage in competition with other stores.

The Court held, in this case as in the other three cases, decided on the same day, that although originally the Sunday Closing Laws were intended to benefit Christianity, in time these laws became secular enactments, and as such are constitutional; they do not violate the Establishment Clause of the First Amendment, which requires the separation of church and state. But does the statute infringe the religious freedom of the plaintiffs?

The Court, in an opinion by Chief Justice Warren, held that the compulsory Sunday closing law does not force anyone to embrace any religious belief or to say anything that is in conflict with Orthodox Judaism; the statute does not make unlawful any of the Orthodox Jewish practices. The statute does, however, make the practice of Orthodox Judaism more expensive for those Jews who believe it necessary to keep their shops closed on both Saturdays and Sundays.

The statute, Warren said, imposes a burden on the plaintiffs' religion indirectly. The statute, however, was not adopted for the purpose of achieving this indirect result. The Court said:

> If the purpose or effect of a law is to impede the observance of one or all religions or is to discriminate invidiously between religions, that law is constitutionally invalid even though the burden may be characterized as being only indirect. But if the State regulates conduct by enacting a general law within its power, the purpose and effect of which is to advance the State's secular goals, the statute is valid despite its indirect burden on religious observance unless the State may accomplish its purpose by means which do not impose such a burden.

The Court considered the question whether the legislature could have accomplished the purpose of the statute and yet have exempt from the law businesses that were closed on Saturdays for religious reasons, and concluded that it was reasonable for the legislature to decide against making exceptions.

The decision was 6-3; Justice Douglas dissented, arguing that the Sunday Closing Laws violated both the Establishment Clause and the Religious Liberty Clause. Justice Brennan (with Justice Stewart concurring with him) dissented only on the ground that by not exempting a business that was closed on Saturdays for religious reasons, the statute violated the Religious Liberty Clause. I will concentrate on the Brennan dissenting opinion.

Justice Brennan put the issue bluntly: "whether a State may put an individual to a choice between his business and his religion. The Court today holds that it may. But I dissent, believing that such a law prohibits the free exercise of religion."

Brennan attacked the way the majority approached the constitutional question. Should a Sunday Closing Law be tested by the minimal requirements of the simple rationalist test, that is, whether the law is rationally related to a legitimate legislative end. Brennan contended that a much more rigorous test must be applied to a statute that infringes on an individual's religious observance. Quoting Justice Jackson's opinion in the Second *Flag Salute Case*, Brennan said that a restriction on a First Amendment freedom could be justified only "to prevent grave and immediate danger to interests which the State may lawfully protect." Religious freedom is, said Brennan, one of the highest values of our society. In effect, the dissent contended that the Pennsylvania law was subject to the strict scrutiny test, and that under this test it would be declared to be unconstitutional.

The effect of the statute was that Orthodox Jews "may not simultaneously practice their religion and their trade, without being hampered by a substantial competitive disadvantage. Their effect [the effect of such laws] is that no one may at one and the same time be an Orthodox Jew and compete effectively with his Sunday-observing fellow tradesmen." Brennan asked pointedly: "What overbalancing need is so weighty in the constitutional scale that it justifies this substantial, though indirect, limitation of appellants' freedom?" It was a rhetorical question. "In fine, the Court...has exalted administrative convenience to a constitutional level high enough to justify making one religion economically disadvantageous." Brennan called the Court's attention to the fact that of the thirty-four States that had Sunday Closing Laws, twenty-one make exemptions, and there is no evidence that those States are significantly noisier on Sundays or that their police are significantly more burdened on account of the exemptions.

V

What was Justice Frankfurter's position in these Sunday Closing Laws Cases? This, of course, is the reason for our present interest in them.

Frankfurter was not satisfied to merely join with the five other Justices who upheld the constitutionality of the statutes; be took the time and trouble to write one of the longest opinions in the Supreme Court Reports, 100 pages and 141 footnotes, in which he laboriously traced the history of such laws, that were originally called Lord's Day laws. He traced their history through English law, through continental law, the American colonial period, and all American States, and the international labor organization, all directed to show that a legislature is not required by the Constitution of the United States to make room for Orthodox Jews or Seventh Day Adventists who observe Saturday as their Sabbath. He found reason to agree with any legislature that would consider any possible objection to the exclusion of an exemption provision and would decide to reject the objection, for whatever reason. On page after page Frankfurter wrote about Orthodox Jews and their grievance against the laws, only to deny their validity under the Free Exercise Clause. At one point he even suggested that if these Sabbatarians were allowed to open their shops on Sundays, they might have a great advantage over their Christian competitors, who would then have cause to complain of discrimination against Christians and Christianity!

It is obvious that Justices Brennan and Stewart, as well as Justice Douglas, had learned more from the history of the persecution of Jews, and of the history of religious persecution, than had Justice Frankfurter. What kept him from drawing the correct constitutional inferences? What kept Frankfurter from fulfilling the great promise with which he took the seat on the Supreme Court on which Cardozo and Holmes had sat before him? He had a mind, intelligence, not at all inferior to theirs, and was not inferior to either of them in scholarship, in learning, in knowledge.

Justice Brennan pointed to a significant difference between the majority's approach (particularly Frankfurter's) and his own. The former saw the need, the public, social need, for a weekly day of rest, and considered the conveniences which led the legislature to select Sunday as such a day of rest and quiet for everyone. However, said

Brennan, be would approach the case differently, "from the point of view of the individuals whose liberty is concededly curtailed by these enactments. For the values of the First Amendment...look primarily towards the preservation of personal liberty, rather than towards the fulfillment of collective goals."

This insight into the jurisprudential difference between the majority's, Frankfurter's, approach and his own connects neatly with the observation of Professor Hoffer, that Frankfurter acted on the Court out of his deep consciousness of the rabbinical fidelity to the idea of obligations, not rights but duties. It was the civic obligation of the Orthodox Jewish merchants to keep their shops closed on Sundays, just as it was their religious obligation, their religious duty to keep them closed on the Jewish Sabbath. They should not think of their rights but of their duties. Frankfurter in his opinions in the *Flag Salute Cases* as well as in the *Sunday Closing Law Cases* expressed a fear of individualism, a fear of trusting one's conscience, a fear that he shared with Edmund Burke who saw that trust in an individual's "private stock of reason" would lead to the commonwealth crumbling away, "be disconnected into the dust and powder of individuality." Holmes, Brandeis, and Cardozo would have been baffled by Frankfurter's perverted view of American individualism. Had they remonstrated, what would he have said? In his headstrong way, he would have said to them: "This is my opinion, not yours."

In 1990, decades after Frankfurter's life had ended, the Court made his opinion theirs as well, and held that a generally applicable criminal law, as long as it was not a law specifically intended to regulate religious belief or practice, need not be justified, under the Free Exercise of Religion Clause of the First Amendment, by a showing that the legislature had a "compelling governmental interest" to adopt the law. Such a law is not subject to the test of "strict scrutiny" despite its burdening a particular religious practice.[9]

Religious groups and civil liberties organizations were justly alarmed by this ruling and clamored Congress to pass legislation overturning the Court's decision, and so in 1943, Congress passed the Religious Freedom Restoration Act,[10] for the purpose of restoring the compelling interest test as set forth in several precedents[11], and to guarantee its application in all cases where free exercise of religion is substantially burdened. Government, declared the statute, may burden a person's exercise of religion only if the government demonstrates that the burden to a person is in furtherance of a compelling governmental interest and is the least restrictive means of furthering that interest. In 1997, however, the Supreme Court declared the act unconstitutional. Justices O'Connor, Breyer, and Souter dissented.[12] In 1999 the House by a vote of 306 to 118, passed the Religious Liberty Protection Act with language that it expected to overcome the Court's objections to the 1993 act. It is doubtful, however, if the later act, if passed also by the Senate, will be acceptable to the Court.

And so, notwithstanding the Free Exercise Clause in the First Amendment, the constitutional law stands as it was formulated by Frankfurter in the *Sunday Closing Law Cases* and in the first *Flag Salute Case* and in the strong, emotionally tinged, memorable dissenting opinion in the second *Flag Salute Case*. If Frankfurter were alive in the 1990s, he would be justified if he felt that, at last, he had been vindicated. But I am not persuaded, for his rise was at the cost of the decline and fall of the Free Exercise Clause, a fundamental, indispensable constitutional guarantee and basic human right.

Notes

1. *Mineraville School Dist. v. Gobitis*, 310 a. a. 586 (1940).
2. *West Virginia State Bd. of Education v. Barnette*, 319 U.S. 624 (1943) .
3. *Lochner v. New York*, 198 U.S. 45 (1905).
4. *Abrams v. U.S.*, 250 U.S. 616 (1919).
5. *Palko v. Conn.*, 302 U.S. 319 (1937).
6. *U.S. v. Carolene Products Co.*, 323 U.S. 18 (1944).
7. *Kovacks v. Cooper*, 336 U.S. 77 (1949)
8. *McGowan v. Maryland*, 366 U.S. 420 (1961); *Braunfeld v. Brown*, 366 U.S. 599 (1961); *Gallagher v. Crown Kosher Super Market*, 366 U. S. 617 (1961); *Two Guys from Harrison v. McGinley*, 366 U. S. 582 (1961).
9. *Employment Division, Oregon Human Resources Dept. v. Smith*, 494 U.S. 872 (1990).
10. 42 U.S.C. 2000bb (1993).
11. *Sherbert v. Verner*, 374 U.S. 398 (1963), *Wisconsin v. Yoder*, 406 U.S. 205 (1972).
12. *City of Boerne v. Flores*, 117 S. Ct. 2157 (1997).

Part 3

Rabbis

7

Leo Jung

Leo Jung (1892-1987) was one of the first English-speaking Orthodox rabbis in the United States. As rabbi of the Jewish Center in New
York for over a half-century and as professor of Jewish ethics at
Yeshiva University for nearly four decades, he played an important
part in fashioning the persona of the modern or centrist Orthodox
American rabbi and in the cultivation of the philosophy of *Torah im-
derkh eretz* or *Torah u-Madda*, the belief that the study of general
culture (literature, philosophy, history, science) should be combined
with study of Torah—the philosophy on which Yeshiva University
and Bar-Ilan University are based. Although in his younger years he
was a leading member and officer of Agudat Israel, for most of his
life he was active on behalf of religious Zionism and the State of
Israel, and played a prominent role in the rescue of Jews from Europe
in the 1930s and 1940s. He wrote and edited numerous works, and
translated and edited two volumes of the Soncino Talmud. Part I of
this essay was published in *Midstream* (August-September 1993).

*   *   *

I

Leo Jung was born in Hungary in 1892. His father[1] emigrated to
England in 1912 to become chief minister, as the position was called,
of the London Federation of Synagogues, comprised of fifty-one congregations that were more Orthodox than those under the chief rabbi
of the United Hebrew Congregations. Leo Jung prepared himself for

the rabbinate by study in various yeshivot and was ordained by three leading rabbis, including Rabbi Abraham Isaac Kook, who during World War I was in London. What was especially important to him was that for three years he studied in the Hildesheimer Rabbinical Seminary in Berlin that was famous for being Modern Orthodox. Simultaneously he studied philosophy, Semitic and classical languages, and other subjects at the universities of Vienna, Berlin, Cambridge, and London. He received his Ph.D. degree in 1922 from the University of London. With this background, it is easy to see how it was that Rabbi Jung (like his father before him) was a strong proponent of the philosophy of *Torah im Derekh Eretz* or *Torah u-Madda*, the study of Torah together with history, science, philosophy, literature, and other secular fields of knowledge, the philosophy of Jewish education generally associated with Samson Raphael Hirsch, and in our day with the position of Yeshiva University, Bar-Ilan University, and Rabbi Dr. J.B. Soloveitchik. Rabbi Jung's personal models for the Jewish educational ideal were the Hildesheimer Seminary in Berlin and the yeshiva in Frankfurt of which Solomon Breuer, Hirsch's son-in-law, was the head.

In 1920 Rabbi Jung accepted an invitation to become the rabbi of a leading Orthodox congregation in Cleveland, a position that had been offered to his father but not accepted by him. Two years later he left Cleveland to become rabbi of the Jewish Center in New York. The center had been founded only a few years before, in 1916, and had still to become a highly regarded congregation. Rabbi Jung was a young man of thirty. For the next sixty-five years his name and that of the Jewish Center were intimately, inextricably connected. Rabbi Jung proved to be the right man at the right place at the right time. After his retirement he was succeeded first by Rabbi Dr. Norman Lamm. When Rabbi Lamm became president of Yeshiva University, he was succeeded by Rabbi Dr. Jacob J. Schacter. Both successors carried on the philosophy and tradition of Rabbi Jung. Rabbi Schacter was also editor of the *Torah u-Madda Journal*, published by Yeshiva University. The interconnections and the influence and legacy of Rabbi Jung are obvious.

As a congregational rabbi, Rabbi Jung imposed on himself limitless involvements. He and Mrs. Jung probably knew each member by name, and they knew their families, and their problems and troubles, which they tried to alleviate. In his sermons, he was ever the teacher and in them as easily and comfortably referred to secular thinkers as to traditional Jewish sages. Rabbi Jung, needless to say, was of course impeccably Orthodox in observances and the performance of mitzvot, but in his sermons placed much more stress on ethics than on ritual. Some members, if consulted, would have preferred a more even distribution. Since the membership of the center was largely middle class, Rabbi Jung especially stressed business ethics, and in his later years wrote more extensively on this subject than on any other aspect of ethics. He was constantly worried lest a prominent Jewish business-man would commit an offense that would cause a *hillul ha-Shem*, a desecration of the Name. In the synagogue, during services, he insisted on the utmost decorum, and that the physical appearance of place and worshippers should manifest the sanctity of beauty no less than the beauty of sanctity. In his writing, he took pains to achieve an impeccable style that reflected his years of study in England, especially Cambridge, and this was equally true of his sermons and conversation. This characteristic did not impress one as contrived or put on, it seemed quite natural and altogether correct; one felt that this was Rabbi Dr. Leo Jung speaking or writing; he could not be judged by someone else's standard of what was proper. He set the standard for others. Like Queen Christina, wherever Rabbi Jung sat, there was the head of the table.

Notwithstanding his heavy involvement with the pastoral and other duties as rabbi of the Jewish Center, Rabbi Jung assumed many communal responsibilities. He was widely known and universally respected, for he did not carry his responsibilities lightly; he accomplished what he undertook. As a Modern or Centrist Orthodox rabbi, his interests were secular as well as religious. He had no hesitation in working with Reform or Conservative rabbis and laymen on common causes. In this Rabbi Jung, as in so many other matters, was something of a pioneer, and set a pattern that others later followed. I can mention only a few of these interests and activities.

In 1926, Rabbi Jung became a member of the Cultural-Religious commission of the American Jewish Joint Distribution Committee, and in 1941 became its chairman, a position that he held for decades. As chairman, he attended countless regular and special meetings and traveled to many parts oft the world to check on how the funds were being used by the religious, educational, and cultural institutions that the JDC supported. This work involved him in very heavy correspondence with persons all over the world. As representative of the JDC, he was especially interested in helping yeshivot in Israel, and he developed a particulars concern for the yeshivot hesder, the Yeshivot B'nai Akiva, that permit their students to serve in the Israel Defense Forces, the yeshiva high schools for boys, and the yeshiva high schools for girls. He also worked assiduously on behalf of Otzar Hatorah, a network of Orthodox day schools in North Africa that combined religious education with vocational training. Similarly, he devoted himself to the support of the Beth Jacob girl schools in Eastern and Central Europe, where thousands of girls were given an education that combined religious, secular, and vocational training.

Rabbi Jung's rescue efforts during World War II deserve special mention. In this he worked alone as well as with relief organizations. "He appealed from the pulpit," records Dr. Raphael, "wrote personal letters, and made house calls to convince congregants to guarantee room and board, as well as temporary living expenses pending employment, for a refugee. He personally collected more than 1,200 affidavits that led to the rescue of over 9,000 Jews."[2] It is doubtful if any American Jew did nearly as much by personal, individual effort.

During the war, Rabbi Jung represented the Orthodox rabbinate on the chaplaincy committee of the Jewish Welfare Board. On this committee he worked with a Reform rabbi and a Conservative rabbi to prepare a prayer book that would be used by all Jewish servicemen— no mean achievement. In addition, he served on the JWB Responsa Committee, together with (Reform) Rabbi Solomon B. Freehof and (Conservative) Rabbi Milton Steinberg, to answer Jewish legal questions from Jewish chaplains and servicemen. Not many Orthodox rabbis would have had the courage to undertake such an assignment, one that Rabbi Jung was able to fulfill with remarkable delicacy of feeling and mutuality of respect.

One can mention only in passing Rabbi Jung's work on behalf of kashrut supervision under the Kosher food law of the State of New York; his organizing the Brith Milah Board of New York and the first hospital training school for mohalim at Mount Sinai Hospital.

During the McCarthy period, Rabbi Jung urged his congregants and Americans generally to repeal the notorious McCarran Internal Security Act and served as vice chairman of the National Committee to Repeal the McCarran Act, and worked vigorously for congress to disband the House Un-American Activities Committee.

Notwithstanding all this work—congregational, national, and international in its reaches and effects—Rabbi Jung never forgot that as a rabbi he was primarily a teacher. He was author or editor of no less than thirty-seven books. Many of them, published by the Soncino Press, are still in print. An especially notable scholarly accomplishment is his translation and annotation of the tractate Yoma of the Babylonian Talmud for the Soncino edition of the Talmud. Ten years after completing this work. Rabbi Jung also translated and annotated the tractate Arakkin.

One of Rabbi Jung's strongest and most enduring loyalties was to Yeshiva University, and his long association with Yeshiva was a constant source of satisfaction to him. Early in 1931, Rabbi Dr. Bernard Revel, founder and president, invited Rabbi Jung to offer a course in ethics at the recently founded Yeshiva College. Rabbi Jung offered a two-semester course in which he delivered four lectures a week, in the first semester on ethics in general, in which he discussed Aristotle, Kant, and other philosophers, and in the second semester he discussed Maimonides, Albo, and other classical Jewish philosophers. Many of his lectures later found themselves in essays and books. His lectures, Dr. Raphael has noted, left "a strong impression on at least two generations of Yeshiva College students"—many of whom became rabbis.

In 1925—that was only three years after Rabbi Jung had come to New York and assumed the position of rabbi at the Jewish Center—he organized the Rabbinical Council, that was to serve as an organization of rabbis ordained by the rabbinical seminary affiliated with Yeshiva and some other English-speaking rabbis, and to be associated with the Kashrut supervision services provided by the Union of Orthodox Jewish Congregations. For ten years, to 1934, Rabbi Jung was chairman of the council; then the council became an independent organization under the name of the Rabbinical Council of America.

I have left for last a discussion of Rabbi Jung's complicated relation to Zionism and Israel because Zionism was also the end of his quest for a meaningful Jewish life. While the true nature of things lies behind and above their appearance, and beyond time and space, Israel and the ideals it represents are in time and in space, yet stand for hopes and strivings that reach far beyond time and space. Rabbi Jung's father was the head of the Agudat Israel in England. The Agudah was founded in 1912 by European Orthodox religious leaders, heads of yeshivot, and hasidic rebbes, including followers of Samson Raphael

Hirsch, all of whom, in various degrees, believed that one could be a full, total Jew as well in Vilna or Budapest as in Jerusalem or Haifa. Jews, they believed, had no need of a Jewish state, and if there was to be a Jewish state, it ought to be ruled by Torah and not by secularist Zionists.

This ideology had a great appeal to Rabbi Leo Jung. He became a leading figure in the Agudah Movement. In 1923, a year after he became rabbi of the Jewish Center, he wrote, "I am not a Zionist." He went on to explain that this did not mean that he was opposed to the upbuilding of Palestine; on the contrary, he said that he wanted a Jewish Eretz Yisrael with all his heart, but one based on Jewish law. He worked tirelessly on behalf of Orthodox schools and other institutions in Palestine that were free of the taint of the godlessness that he associated with the Zionists. He, however, stressed his firm belief that Judaism and Jewish law must not be forced upon the Jews in Palestine, not any more than on Jews in the United States.

Rabbi Jung's anti-Zionism was, however, not absolute. It was influenced by the fact that his father had joined Rabbi Abraham Isaac Kook in traveling throughout England to secure thousands of signatures in favor of the Foreign Office's pending Balfour Declaration. My personal opinion is that Rabbi Leo Jung was attracted to the Agudat Israel, not by its opposition to Zionism, but by the fact that it was headed by rabbis and heads of yeshivot for whom he had the deepest respect. He thought of them as great saints and sages. He felt awed and honored to be associated with them. This was a feeling that he never lost. To the end of his days he commissioned and collected biographical papers on these great scholars and teachers and published them in books. With this strong feeling of loyalty to leaders of the movement, he readily accepted the position of chief secretary for the Agudah's first Kenessiah Gedolah (Great Conference) in Vienna in 1923, and some fifteen years later arranged that the first meeting to establish a foundation for Agudat Israel in the United States would be held at the Jewish Center.

But in the early 1940s strains developed between Rabbi Jung and Agudah leadership. For some Agudah rabbis, Rabbi Jung was too modern, too liberal; he was not, for them, strict enough in his interpretation of ritual law, he was not ultra-orthodox and associated too freely with Reform and Conservative rabbis and laymen. At one time he tried to bring together Mizrachi and Agudah, at least on a common educational program. This alone was enough to subject him to suspicion.

After V-E day the rift widened, "Dissatisfied with some of Agudah's 'morally doubtful emissaries,' the ethically sensitive Jung also found it hard to tolerate," Dr. Penkower wrote, "the cynicism and double-dealing to be found within the movement's high echelons, both in America and in Palestine."[3] The break became inevitable. He moved closer to Rabbi Kook's Zionist philosophy, and accepted an invitation to become a member of the enlarged Jewish Agency. The Jewish Center celebrated Zion Flag Day, Rabbi Jung hailed the Balfour Declaration, his congregation raised money for the Jewish National Fund. Gradually, Rabbi Jung had moved away from Agudat Israel toward Poalei Agudah, which more readily supported the Jewish nationalist movement. When the U.N. General Assembly in 1947 voted in favor of a Jewish state in a partitioned Palestine, Rabbi Jung rejoiced with tears in his eyes, and wrote, "Now we can smile again, and march again and be Jews again," with no need for apologetics. The State of Israel, he wrote, represented "the perennial hope, promise and eventual consummation of our national hope." He campaigned diligently for the United Jewish Appeal and Israel Bonds and on behalf of Orthodox schools and hospitals, and for vocational training in yeshivot. Rabbi Jung's work on behalf of Israel is properly commemorated by Kfar Eliyahu (his Hebrew name), the first girls' village that has become a vast complex of junior and senior high schools and a teachers' college for Orthodox girls, and by the JNF Forest in Safad bearing the names of Rabbi Leo and Irma Jung.

In his movement away from the anti-Zionism of the Agudah, I believe that Rabbi Jung was influenced by the life and teachings of Chief Rabbi Kook, and by the life and teachings of Rabbi Azriel Hildesheimer, each of whom, in his own way, supported the settlement of Palestine as Eretz Yisrael, the building of the yishuv, the advancement of the ideals of Hovevei Zion, and the colonization movement. And in cooperating with Reform and Conservative rabbis and laymen on behalf of common objectives he also followed the example of Rabbi Hildesheimer.

Although separated from Agudah, Rabbi Jung, however, never lessened his profound veneration of great rabbis, scholars, and heads of yeshivot. I recall the frequent references he made in conversation to Rabbi Dr. Jehiel Jacob Weinberg, renowned talmudist, whom he visited at his yeshiva in Montreux as often as he could and I recall, too, that once when we vacationed together at Grindelwald, he asked me to accompany him as he walked over to the hotel to pay his respect to Rabbi Isaac Hutner, head of the Rabbi Chaim Berlin Yeshiva, whom he esteemed as a great halachist.

All art, Walter Pater said, aspires "towards the condition of music." All life, Rabbi Jung believed, aspires towards the condition of the holy. I think that this was at the heart of his teaching. Man is made in the image of God, but man lives as if he does not know this, and in his ignorance and waywardness he is no better than the stone, which, as Meister Eckhart said, is ignorant of the fact that it is God. Rabbi Jung was constantly aware of the tension between divine immanence and divine transcendence: he was constantly aware of the wonder and beauty of love, and of the ineluctable link between mortality and eternity.

But just as a poem should not mean but be, so, too, we may say that Rabbi Jung was much more than his works and accomplishments. He was a fine example of the unusual fusion of the outer and inner man. He gave the appearance of being tall and stately, and of being immaculately clean in both body and soul. In his dress he accepted the judgment of the talmudic sage who said that a scholar who had a single spot on his cloak deserved harsh punishment at the hands of heaven. He was dignified in his walk no less than in his speech. When he entered a room where there was a gathering, his presence was instantly felt. He once told me that he and Mrs. Jung had established the practice of taking off one day a week, when they would leave their apartment and go off to spend the day at the seaside or in the country-side, or at a museum, and thus invited their souls. He followed the old maxim, "If you have two loaves of bread, sell one and buy a hyacinth for your soul." He made one believe that one has, indeed, a soul, and that the soul needs the nourishment of a hyacinth.

II

Rabbi Jung occupies a notable place in the history of the American rabbinate, for he was one of the first Orthodox rabbis who combined secular scholarship with his rabbinical studies. Overlapping his early years but belonging to an earlier generation were Rabbi Dr. Philip Klein, Rabbi Dr. Bernard Drachman, and Rabbi Dr. Moses Hyamson, who deviated from the normal type of Orthodox rabbi, but they opened no path for others to follow and had only limited influence. Rabbi Jung's influence, however, was far-reaching; he served as a role model for hundreds of rabbis who had been his students, from him they learned that one is not necessarily a heretic if one studies the writings of Aristotle, or Plato, or Kant. They learned from him that Nature, too, discloses the mind of the Creator; as Psalm 19 says, "The heavens declare the glory of God, and the firmament proclaims His handiwork." Rabbi Jung reminded his students that the Talmud insisted that "he who had a chance to study the cosmos and failed to do so, belonged to sinners who would not look upon the world of God."[4] Not only is there no conflict between Judaism and science, Judaism considers scientific study as another way of studying the mind of God. Moreover, as the *Amidah* (the central weekday prayer) says, "*Atoh honen le-adam da'at*," "Thou graciously endows *man* with intelligence, and Thou teaches mortal *man* to have knowledge and understanding."[5] God endowed Adam and Eve, and all their progeny—not only the children of Israel—with a capacity to seek and acquire knowledge and understanding.

And so it was quite natural for Rabbi Jung to quote from the writings of Goethe and Lessing, from Ibsen, Lincoln, Newton, Gandhi, Seneca, and even Saint Augustine, with the same ease and grace as when he referred to the thoughts of Rashi or Maimonides.[6]

There are today—unfortunately—rabbis and teachers at yeshivas who discourage their students from studying secular subjects (apart from those indispensable for making a living). Rabbi Jung, however, was a strong proponent of Yeshiva University, and was among the first to support Yeshiva College when it was founded in the late 1920s. He believed that one has not only the right, but has the duty to seek knowledge wherever it may be found, in the library or in the laboratory, in the college or the yeshiva.[7] He maintained that for Judaism the study of medicine symbolizes the sacredness of the material world that God had created. Thus according to the Talmud, a scholar should choose to live in a city only if it has a physician and a surgeon. It is no wonder that Maimonides, Nachmanides, Judah Halevi, and many of the great scholars mentioned in the Talmud were physicians, for whom medicine was not merely a means of making a living, but a spiritual calling. To Leo Jung, therefore, it was altogether fitting that Yeshiva University should found the Einstein College of Medicine, that exists alongside the Rabbi Isaac Elkanan Theological Seminary, Yeshiva College, Stern College, and schools for other professions and disciplines.

Rabbi Jung remembered that his father's library included, alongside the great works of Judaism, the classics of general literature and of philosophy, in a variety of languages, from many nations, and observed that ancient Greek thinkers and nineteenth-century philosophers "had a place in the heart of the enlightened father [as in the heart] of the aspiring son." All his life he was aware that there is in Judaism a broad and deep humanistic spirit, so that it was natural that the beauty of Japheth should be found in the tents of Shem.[8]

It is important, I think, to note that Rabbi Jung did not believe that sacred and secular studies exist merely side by side, as neighbors, as parallel lines of learning. Not at all! these studies must be intertwined, they must interact, for there is only one mind, and there are no walls within the mind. This is what *Torah u-Madda*, what *Torah im derech eretz* meant to Rabbi Jung. Worldly culture is not a frosting on the cake. It is part of "the Torah's emphatic and persistent accent on truth, justice, compassion, and the work for peace." Rabbi Jung agreed—passionately agreed—with the teaching of Maharal miPrag:

> It is in order to study the wisdom of the nations. Why should one not study this wisdom which derives from God, since the wisdom of the nations also derives from God? It is He who imparted to them of His wisdom. ...It is proper for a person to study whatever sheds light on the nature of the world, *and he is obliged to do so*. Everything is God's creation, and it is in order to investigate it, so that thereby [it becomes possible] to understand the Creator.

This was a central teaching of Rabbi Jung.

From these basic beliefs, it is not surprising that Rabbi Jung held that Jews must not isolate themselves in a self-imposed ghetto and cut themselves off from the rest of mankind but must seek links of fellowship with the wise and the righteous of all nations.[9] Rabbi Jung belonged to the school of Rabbi Meier, who stated that a gentile who occupies himself with the study of Torah is equal in status to that of the High Priest.[10] Since all men, of whatever race or nationality, are fashioned in the image of their Creator, all men must be respected; to dishonor one is to dishonor the Creator. "I have always viewed my Jewish duty," said Rabbi Jung, "as covering relations not only with members of my own people but with everyone of God's children." Citing Maimonides, he contended that to both Jew and Christian "belongs the glory and the task of hastening the advent of the Messiah."[11]

There are, he believed, "many ways to God," and that both Jews and Christians are on the earth to stay. He said that God's love, and its emanation in the love that is inherent in the soul of man, knows no limitation by race, geography, or social status. He cited, with apparent approval, the action of Rabbi Sadia Gaon who eliminated from the morning liturgy the passage that says, "O cause a new light to shine on Zion"—*ohr hodosh al-tzion toeer*—"for the prayer was addressed to the Universal Giver of Light and should not be narrowed to the light of Zion." Rabbi Jung interpreted the *sephirat ha-omer*, the counting of forty-nine days between Passover and Shvuot, as a counting of days not only for the Jewish people but for the human race, for they represent the Messianic hope, not only for the Jews but for all God's children.

From these beliefs, Rabbi Jung concluded that inter-faith amity "must not be viewed as peripheral, temporal, or seasonal. It goes to the core of spiritual sincerity." Interdenominational actions were to him not a matter of mere public relations but were an integral part of Judaism. Working in common with others for the commonwealth was a religious duty. The same spirit animated Rabbi Jung to work with other Jews, regardless of religious differences, for common causes. He maintained that Jewish interdenominational respect and friendship are requirements of Jewish law. "American Jews must recognize the necessity of cooperation [among themselves] without compromise."[13] Rabbi Jung may have been the only rabbi who ventured to say, let the Conservative Jew see to it that the members of *his* group be loyal to Conservative Judaism, and let the Reform Jew see to it that Reform Jews do not stray away from Judaism, and let the Orthodox Jew attack the ignorance and indifference that can be found within the Orthodox community. If each would hold fast to the demands of righteousness, the face of American Jewry would be infinitely brighter and its future would be full of promise.

God, according to Rabbi Jung, "lets our free will have its full sway." He reminds us that it was not God, but men, who built the munitions factories and manufactured poison gas. "It is not He who has failed us." He often quoted the saying of Goethe that we must *think* as if we were in the ideal world but must *work* as in the real world. And the real world was left unfinished by the Creator. God, as a morning prayer states, daily renews the work of creation.[14] "God's love of man," Rabbi Jung wrote, "manifested itself in that He did not present him with a ready-to-use world but with an emergent creation." The earth was both a gift and a task, and we are placed on it with work to do. Rabbi Jung interpreted a passage in *Pirke Avot* as meaning, "None is free who does not serve the ideal." Every action should therefore be performed sacramentally. Not only the material world, but also the spiritual world, including Torah, is an emerging world. Through interpretation, Torah becomes renewed and recreated. Revelation did not take place at Sinai once for all time, it continues to take place daily. The spirit can open itself to the reception of divine teaching.

Rabbi Jung brought the philosophy of pragmatism to bear on Judaism. The proposition *Ani mamin*, "I believe in perfect faith" is not a statement of fact but is a promise and a prayer or plea—"I shall believe. I should believe. My life must make my belief come true." So, too, the proposition, "I am the Lord thy God" is not a statement of fact but is a commandment that says, "I shall believe in God. I shall make Him the standard of my life. My life shall make true my belief in God. Each of my daily actions will affirm my belief in God." Only by his life, by his actions, can the Jew prove to himself—and to the world—that his beliefs are indeed true.[15]

A phrase that most frequently was used by Rabbi Jung in his sermons and writings is "Torah-true Judaism." Taken out of context, one may be led to think that the phrase was meant to identify its user as ultra-Orthodox, as one who holds that Judaism can be sustained and observed only when the Jew is isolated, only when the Jewish community is confined within impregnable walls that separate it from the rest of the world. As we have seen, however, this would be a misreading of Rabbi Jung's character and teaching. It might have been better if he had used the phrase "Torah-true-u-Madda Judaism." For the connection between Torah and culture is inseparable, as is also the connection between Jew and world, between the sacred and the secular. What Rabbi Jung surely meant was that the Torah must not get lost in the culture, the sacred must not become assimilated into the secular, but, on the contrary, the secular must be raised into the sacred, the culture must become part of Torah.

Ultimately, more important than his teaching, was the man himself. Rabbi Jung was a person who had succeeded to mould his life into an artistic design that united the twelve moral and intellectual virtues of Aristotle with the spirituality of Judaism. His personality and character were an embodiment of the Jewish ideal of *hadrat kodesh,* of the beauty of holiness.

Notes

1. For biographical facts concerning Leo Jung, see *Reverence, Righteousness, and Rahamanut,* edited by Jacob J. Schacter, especially the essays by Marc Lee Raphael and Monty N. Penkower (Jason Aronson, 1992); *The Path of a Pioneer: The Autobiography of Leo Jung* (Soncino Press, 1980); *The Leo Jung Jubilee Volume,* edited by M.M. Kasher, Norman Lamm, Leonard Rosenfeld (Jewish Center, 1962), especially the essay by Nima Adlerblum.
2. *Reverence, Righteousness, and Rahamnut,* 57.
3. Ibid., 219.
4. *The Path of a Pioneer,* 139, 144.
5. *Authorized Daily Prayer Book* (S. Singer), (London, 1962), 48.
6. Leo Jung, *Studies in Torah Judaism: Knowledge and Love in Rabbinic Lore* (Yeshiva University Press, 1963), 22.
7. *The Path of a Pioneer,* 45, 69.
8. Ibid., 21. See also Leo Jung, *Crumbs and Character* (Night and Day Press, 1942), 217.
9. *The Path of a Pioneer,* 69; *Studies in Torah Judaism,* 22.
10. Bab. Talmud, Ab. Zar. 3a.
11. *Crumbs and Character,* 17, 85, 86, 90, 92.
12. *Authorized Daily Prayer Book,* 40.
13. *The Path of a Pioneer,* 19, 132. *Crumbs and Character,* 54, 153, 314.
14. *Authorized Daily Prayer Book,* 40.
15. *Crumbs and Character,* 140, 141.

8

Robert Gordis

Robert Gordis (1908-1992), while an active and busy congregational rabbi, was professor of Bible and of Jewish philosophy at the Jewish Theological Seminary and visiting professor at various universities and seminaries, and leading exponent of the philosophy of Conservative Judaism. When, in the 1980s, the Rabbinical Assembly and the Jewish Theological Seminary planned to appoint a commission to formulate a statement of principles of Conservative Judaism they knew that, "for the project to succeed, we needed an outstanding chairman who could command the respect of all participants. One rabbi who stood head and shoulders above others was Rabbi Robert Gordis" (*Emet Ve-Emunah*, 1988, p. 2). In biblical scholarship, his major contribution is his translation of and commentary on various books of the Wisdom section of the Hebrew Bible. Author of over a score of scholarly books, Gordis wrote on religion and contemporary problems, and on the role of Judaism in the modern world, and for forty years he was editor of the quarterly journal *Judaism*, of which he was co-founder.

*　*　*

I

For many years, during the holiday Passover, when the Song of Songs is read in the synagogue, I turned to *The Song of Songs: A Study, Modern Translation and Commentary*, by Robert Gordis, not only to read his wondrously poetic translation and rendition into twenty-eight songs and fragments, but to study his fifteen detailed chapters and the scores of notes in his commentary. Although text and commentary have become familiar to me by an annual rereading since the book's publication in 1954, the book remains an ever-fresh source of literary, religious, intellectual enjoyment. The holiday in 1992 came only several months after the death of Gordis on January 3, and so the sense of bereavement, deprivation, the feeling of heaviness of heart affected my study of the book, and I felt that my mood was more fit for a study of the book of Lamentations than of Song of Songs. The death of Gordis brought to an end a most productive, creative, pulsating life, that of a person who stood tall among his peers, and who will be remembered as one of the outstanding scholars in the field of Jewish studies, whose name will evoke the same respect that we owe to rabbi-scholars like Solomon Schecter, Abraham Joshua Heschel, and Louis Finkelstein.

The words "rabbi-scholar" are intentionally hyphenated, for these men, while preeminent for their meticulous, objective, modest scholarship, were at the same time recognized for their wide communal and leadership qualities as rabbis. Gordis served as rabbi at a large congregation for thirty-eight years. He established the first Conservative all-day school in the United States, now named the Robert Gordis Day School of Belle Harbor. He was president of the Rabbinical Assembly of America and of the Synagogue Council of America. He took an active part in interfaith activities. He was recognized as the leading philosopher of the Conservative movement.

All of this, and much more, can be mentioned about Gordis as a public figure. But there was a quiet side to him that, in my estimation, was even more important. For twenty or more years he was professor of Bible and of philosophy of religion at the Jewish Theological Seminary, where his influence was felt by hundreds of students who became rabbis and scholars. In 1952 he was a co-founder of the quarterly journal *Judaism*, and for two score years he served first as chairman of the board of editors and then as editor. The forty volumes of the journal will stand as a tribute to Gordis's indefatigable energies and creative qualities as editor.

And last but most important of all, there are the twenty or more books that Gordis published, and the numerous scholarly articles that only a professional bibliographer can take into account. The books by Gordis can be, I think, put into two categories. First are his books on the Bible, particularly on the Wisdom books. I have already mentioned his book on the Song of Songs, first published in 1954. In 1973 his treatise on this book was combined with his treatise on Lamentations. In 1965 he published *The Book of God and Man: A Study of Job*; in 1978 this book was replaced by an enlarged edition, *The Book of Job: Commentary, New Translation, and Special Studies*. In 1974 his treatise on the book of Esther was published. His massive study of Ecclesiastes was published in 1951 as *Koheleth—The Man and His World*. These books alone, on five of the Wisdom books of the Bible, will suffice to sustain Gordis's reputation as a master of Bible scholarship, a field of study that has been much more cultivated by Christian than by Jewish scholars. In some respects, Gordis was a pioneer in dedicating himself to Bible studies and has served as a role model for younger Jewish scholars.

When an East European rabbi was told of the magisterial commentary on the Psalms by Samuel Raphael Hirsch, he remarked that the Lithuanian Jews recited the Psalms (*Thillim*) and studied Talmud, but Hirsch recites Talmud and studies *Thillim*. In this respect, *mutatis mutandis*, Gordis was a Hirschian. He tried to reclaim the Bible for respectable Jewish scholarship. For his pragmatic, hardheaded, rational bent of mind that was always attracted to matter-of-factness, the Wisdom books were especially congenial and appealing.

His study of the Wisdom books in depth, however, inevitably gave Gordis insight into many aspects of biblical scholarship in general. At least three of his books resulted from his intensive study; namely, *Biblical Text in the Making*, 1971; *Poets, Prophets and Sages—Essays in Biblical Interpretation*, 1970; and *The Word and the Book—Studies in Biblical Language and Literature*, 1976. Taken together, his eight books on the Bible place Gordis in the very first rank of biblical scholarship and alone will constitute an enduring monument to his eminence and authority.

Gordis's scholarship, as I have said, falls into a second category: his books that manifest his character as rabbi and teacher, the rabbi whose duty it is to teach his congregation, his *edah*, the widely dispersed community of Israel. In these books Gordis addressed many of the issues and problems that modern life has created or accentuated for the Jew who has not been overwhelmed by the secularism that has become pervasive. Into this category fall at least the following eight books: *Judaism for the Modern Age*, 1955; *Root and Branch—Judaism and the Free Society*, 1962; *Judaism in a Christian World*, 1966;

A Faith for Moderns, 1966; *Sex and Family in the Jewish Tradition*, 1967; *Love and Sex—A Modern Jewish Perspective*, 1978; *Judaic Ethics for a Lawless World*, 1986; and his last book, *The Dynamics of Judaism—A Study in Jewish Law*, 1990.

These books reveal a mind that may be best described as Hellenistic, a mind far removed from any suggestion of parochialism; a mind at home in different cultures and civilizations; a person who looks for truth and wisdom wherever they may be found, and who disregards no-trespass signs; a person who can speak of Judaism to Christians and secularists as easily and as comfortably as he can speak to professing Jews. Gordis was an American Jew but also a Jewish American, for he believed in the truth and importance of the Bill of Rights no less than in the truth and importance of the Ten Commandments. He believed in the God of Israel, the God of Abraham, Isaac and Jacob, but also in God who is the creator of Adam and Eve, the progenitors of all mankind, of all men and women made in the image of God. Gordis held firmly to the principle of live and let live; he was tolerant of all things but superstition, cruelty, hatred. He immersed himself often in the study of *halacha*, Jewish law, but he also had great regard for opinions and decisions of the United States Supreme Court, which he studied with open-mindedness and respect. Holding firmly to the Jewish this-worldly affirmation, Gordis with equal firmness held that while the natural is holy as a manifestation of the divine, the existence of the divine draws the spirit toward a transcendental experience that brings a spiritual significance to human experience and life. The Song of Songs, he wrote, "is both the record of God's revelation to man and of man's aspiration toward the Divine."

II

Robert Gordis might well have claimed, with justification, that his last book, *The Dynamics of Judaism—A Study in Jewish Law*, is both a record of God's revelation to him and of his aspiration toward the Divine. For Gordis believed that revelation is "a meeting involving both God and man as active participants."[1] Revelation, he maintained, is dynamic. There is continuity, as a deposit of past revelation, but there is also change, expressive of the newness of revelation.[2] There is constant interpretation of the past and reinterpretation; and both the interpretation and the reinterpretation are "words of the Living God."[3]

The book can justly be read as Robert Gordis's intellectual and religious last will and testament. As the preface states, nearly all the contents of the book were written especially for it. Gordis lived long enough to have completed the manuscript, including the preface, but he unfortunately fell ill while reviewing the edited manuscript. The book was written when Gordis was already an octogenarian, yet at a time when the author enjoyed the mature, full vigor of mind and spirit. I think that as he wrote the book Gordis was happy that he was putting the finishing touches on the labors of his life. He did not try to say anything that he had not said before. He had thought and brooded long and over many years. This is precisely why the book is so important: it is a reaffirmation, a recrudescence of his strongest faith, recorded in his green old age.

Gordis recognized that the book would reflect the character of the author and the nature of his life. It would not, therefore, be a book written in an ivory tower. The author could not claim detachment from his station and its duties; he is dedicated to *Torah lishma*, to learning for its own sake, learning with no ulterior, no practical purpose, *and* to learning for the sake of life, *Torat hayyim*, learning with a pragmatic end in view. It is not easy, or perhaps even possible, always to keep these two activities separated. They often intertwine, for Gordis was no split personality, a scholar in the morning and a famous, busy rabbi in the afternoon. I think that Gordis as a rabbi believed that he also had to be a scholar, and as a scholar believed that he had to be a rabbi. The two callings were in dialectical tension, that was resolved and harmonized by a supervening spirit that made Robert Gordis a whole person, and as such he was the author of *The Dynamics of Judaism: A Study in Jewish Law*.

III

A central thought of the book is that Judaism is not a religion that, in the past, was often identified as the "Mosaic faith." Nor is it the religion of the Mishnah and Talmud. The special character of Judaism is, said Gordis, the fruit of development.[4] Contrary to Arnold Toynbee, Judaism is not a fossilized religion. The "dialectic of continuity and change"[5] has almost always been characteristic of Judaism. What Roscoe Pound said of the law in general may be said of Judaism and of Jewish law: "The law must be stable, but it must not stand still."[6]

This may sound paradoxical, the affirmation of contradictories; but life and the world are not based on the rules of logic; they operate not on the principle of either/or but on the principle of both; and "evermore in the world," said Emerson, "is this marvelous balance of beauty and disgust, magnificence and rats."[7] He might have added "stability and change, permanence and alteration."

Insofar as Judaism is a biblical religion, it developed over the centuries a unique character that differentiated it from all pagan religions. First, Judaism is a faith that represented the commitment of and to an entire people; the covenant is not with any special group, a caste of priests or members of a superior class—"God's covenant encompassed an entire people."[8]

Second, the covenant was and is ethical in character. And third, Israel enjoyed a unique religious leadership in the prophets, whose central demand was for righteousness. The sages and rabbis who followed sought to embody the biblical-prophetic principles of righteousness into *halachah*, the laws and way of life. Because of the loss of the Temple, the sages and rabbis felt that the great need was to preserve Judaism and the Jewish people, and they resorted to an emphasis on rites and ritual—on the ceremonial law—to achieve these ends.[9] Religion, culture, and kinship became interrelated in Judaism. Other ancient peoples also had these three characteristics, but only the Jewish people and Judaism have survived, and Jews continue to constitute a unique people by organically combining these three elements.[10]

The Jewish people have a long history, a religion and a culture that have a very rich past, but not everything in a people's past is usable. At least three principles of Judaism stand out as special from the total tradition and cannot be discarded; they are, above all other aspects of the Jewish tradition, of supreme usefulness, now and ever, and these are: First, the principle that life must be affirmed—"*affirmation of life as a good here and now*, including all its physical and spiritual aspects, and in spite of all its frustrations and agonies."[11] Gordis quoted with eager approval the statement in the Talmud that "every human being is destined to render an account before God for all the blessings of the world that his eyes beheld and he did not enjoy."[12] Second, the principle of self-fulfillment. This flows naturally out of the first principle, the affirmation of life. By self-fulfillment a person affirms his or her life. "If I am not for myself, who will be for me?"[13] "If I am here, all is here, and if I am not here, who is here?"[14] "Love thy neighbor as thyself."[15] One must begin with love of oneself.[16] Just as there are commandments between person and person, and commandments between person and God—*mitzot bein adam lahavero, mitzot bein adam lamakom*—so, too, there are *mitzvot bein adam leazmo*, commandments between person and himself or herself: "the obligation of a human being to preserve his physical and mental well-being and above all to safeguard his personal integrity and purity—in a word, to refrain from sinning against himself." This is a category of commandments that ought to be recognized as existing at the very core of Judaism. Its recognition "would effectively rebut the notion of 'victimless crimes' and stigmatize practices like alcoholism, prostitution, drug abuse, and suicide as infractions of the moral law. Indeed, the Jewish tradition considers the biblical injunction 'Take utmost care and watch yourselves scrupulously' (Deut. 4:9, cf. v. 15) as the basis for the religious duty to take care of one's health and well being."[17]

Just as self-fulfillment flows out of the principle of the affirmation of life, so, too, flows from the commandment of the affirmation of life the principle of social justice. "It is because each human being has a right and a duty to enjoy the blessings of the world that justice is a universal obligation. Injustice in all of its forms means the encroachment by one person or group on the legitimate and inalienable right of another to partake of the joys available in this world, in which all human beings have a share."[18]

As expressive of the spirit of Judaism, Gordis quotes the hasidic rebbe who declared, "Why do you worry about my soul and about your own body? Worry about my body and your own soul!"[19] One may, writes Gordis, accept the opinion of Rabbi Akiba that the Golden Rule of Judaism is the great principle, *kelal gadol*, the commandment, "You shall love your neighbor as yourself"; or one may prefer the statement of Ben Azzai, that the foundational principle of Judaism is the passage in Genesis (5:1): "This is the book of the generations of Adam. When God created man, He made him in the likeness of God; male and female He created them." It does not matter, for there is "no denying that 'the great principle of the Torah' is ethical."[20]

The principle of the affirmation of life, and the principle of self fulfillment—with its implication that the right of self-fulfillment means also the duty of sharing in the blessings of the world, "all unite to establish the ideal of justice as the cornerstone of Jewish ethics."[21]

Yes, justice is the cornerstone of Judaism. Gordis did not tire of emphasizing and restating this principle. *Not love but justice.* Perhaps some persons can feel the emotion of love for people far removed from them, on the other side of the globe, but for mankind in general to use "love" in this way verges on cant. The most that can be demanded "is that we respond to all other human beings in the spirit of justice, no matter how far away or how different they may be. Nor do we require any other standard. Justice is enough. It applies equally to all persons by virtue of their common humanity, their innate dignity as children of God, and their inalienable right to the blessings of life, liberty, and the pursuit of happiness."[22] Even God Himself is bound by the demands of justice ("Far be it from Thee! Shall not the Judge of all the earth do right?" [Gen. 18:25])."Clearly," says Gordis, "justice is the ultimate value to which God's will must conform."[23] "[I]n Jewish tradition and law the ethical is the highest rung on the ladder of faith."[24]

Because, following the destruction of the Temple by the Roman army, the ceremonial law was emphasized as a unifying force for the Jewish people, the impression may have been created that rites and rituals are all-important. They are, indeed, important, says Gordis, "But what of the relative importance of ritual and ethics in Judaism? .... Here the evidence in both the Bible and the Talmud, though often overlooked, is extensive and unequivocal—ritual is important but ethics is paramount."[25]

In the liturgy of Yom Kippur, the central feature is the recital of the *al het,* the "great confession." Gordis calls attention to the fact that forty offenses are listed, "all are ethical sins, not one a ritual transgression."[26]

In view of the centrality of ethics, justice, and righteousness, it is not surprising that Gordis should give to the status of women in Jewish law more extensive consideration than to any other feature of *halachah.* He believed that the "greatest revolution" of modern times is the change in the status of women.[27] In view of the fact that women constitute at least one-half of the world's population, Gordis may well be right. He finds many things that need correction: indignities, injustices, improprieties, and humiliations that cry for removal or correction. But Gordis was not one who despaired. As a scholar who was intimately aware of all the legal details and the wrongs that need amelioration, he also saw that the Jewish tradition had a trend in the right direction. "It is not strange," he wrote, "that women began with many disabilities. What is remarkable is the ongoing effort in Judaism to enlarge their rights and opportunities and to limit the powers and prerogatives of men, a pattern that may be traced from the biblical and rabbinic periods to the present."[28] One of the most interesting and useful aspects of *The Dynamics of Judaism* is the documentation that it provides to prove the correctness of this far-reaching judgment.

Gordis's approach to the problem of women and to *halachah* in general reminds me of William James's statement that he was not an optimist and not a pessimist but one who believed in amelioration. Nothing is inevitable, and the possibility of improvement is ever present. Gordis was a meliorist, for that is what Judaism imposes upon its adherents. The people of Israel are commanded to act *mipnei tikkun haolam,* "for the improvement of society," for the correction of the unfinished world, for doing the work that the Creator left undone.[29] The Jew "comes [into the world] with work to do, he does not come to coo."[30]

But meliorism implicates change, improvement on an existing situation; something is wrong that calls for replacement with something that is better. Judaism involves the use of two forces to accomplish a change for the better; namely, reason and moral conscience, both of them attributes that are *helek Eloah mimmaal*, "a portion from God above."[31] "Throughout Jewish history," says Gordis:

> these two great canons of reason and moral conscience have been the means by which Jewish leadership received the traditional inheritance of the past and preserved it for the future. In the majority of instances, the tradition could be and was maintained with little or no change. But when change became necessary, the Rabbis did not hesitate to evaluate the tradition and modify it before handing it over to their successors. They recognized that successive generations of scholars were not merely repeating traditions and decisions from the past, but were revealing new and unfamiliar aspects of the Torah. It is not without interest that the comments of scholars on the work of their predecessors are called *hiddushim*, "novellae," "new interpretations."[32]

The rabbis and sages firmly believed that the Torah embodied "the highest spiritual and ethical values," and therefore they did not hesitate to interpret the Bible "freely, invoking one procedure in one case and a diametrically opposite one in another, depending on the goal they sought to achieve,"[33] and the goal was always justice, righteousness, an ethical value.

A large part of *The Dynamics of Judaism* discusses numerous instances of this process of ameliorating *halachahic* decisions and legislation, and the possibility of using the processes of reason and the moral conscience, especially in the area of the status of women. This aspect of the work happily makes the book itself a *hiddush*, a new, creative interpretation, by one who had a deeply pious regard for tradition; a tradition that contains in itself a program and a process for change that will bear witness to both reason and the demands of the moral conscience. It is a work of consequence, written by a choice and master spirit of our age. A man wrote it whose life, character and mind reflect an intense and life-long study of the Wisdom books of the Bible.

Notes

1. *The Dynamics of Judaism: A Study in Jewish Law* (Bloomington: Indiana University Press, 1990), 82.
2. Ibid., 75.
3. Ibid., 96.
4. Ibid., 2
5. Ibid., 75.
6. Roscoe Pound, *Introduction to the Philosophy of Law* (1922),
7. Emerson, *The Conduct of Life* (1860), VII.
8. *Dynamics of Judaism*, note 1, p. 2.
9. Ibid., 4.
10. Ibid.
11. Ibid., 15. Emphasis in original.
12. Ibid., 16. P. Kiddushin, at end.
13. Hillel, Avot 1:14.
14. Hillel, Sukkah 53a.
15. Levit. 19:18.
16. Cf. Erich Fromm, *The Art of Loving* (1957), 60 ff.
17. *Dynamics of Judaism*, note 1, pp. 21, 33, 63.
18. Ibid., 22.
19. Ibid.
20. Ibid., 123.
21. Ibid., 23.
22. Ibid., 25.
23. Ibid., 67.
24. Ibid., 68.
25. Ibid., 64
26. Ibid., 87.
27. Ibid., 145.
28. Ibid., 149.
29. Ibid., 124.
30. "Peace," by Gerard Manley Hopkins.
31. *Dynamics of Judaism*, note 1, p. 80.
32. Ibid.
33. Ibid., 81.

9

Jacob B. Agus

Jacob B. Agus (1911-1986) was a leading scholar in the field of the philosophy of Judaism of the twentieth century. As a graduate student of religion at Harvard, Professor William Ernest Hocking influenced him. Notwithstanding his active life as a congregational rabbi and as a professor at Temple University, Dropsie College and other institutions of higher learning, he was an author of many works, including a full-scale study of Rabbi Abraham Isaac Kook. In his book *Modern Philosophies of Judaism*, he included critical studies of Hermann Cohen, Martin Buber, Franz Rosenzweig, and Mordecai M. Kaplan. He participated in interfaith work, and as part of this interest he acted as consultant on Judaism for the *Encyclopedia Britannica*, and contributed to the *Catholic Theological Encyclopedia*. He conducted a notable correspondence with Arnold Toynbee about Judaism, some of which Toynbee published in his volume *Reconsiderations*, that is volume 12 of his *Study of History*. He was also highly regarded for his contributions to the development of a philosophy of the Conservative Movement in Judaism. See *American Rabbi: The Life and Thought of Jacob B. Agus*, edited by Steven T. Katz (1997).

*　　*　　*

Writing about the work of David Neumark, Jacob Agus said that although Neumark's contributions to the study of Jewish philosophy are invaluable, he, however, never became an independent philosopher.[1] One can say of Agus himself that his contributions to the study of Jewish philosophy are invaluable, and that he himself became an independent philosopher. Very few scholars were as deeply immersed in the study and interpretation of Jewish philosophy, from Philo to Rosenzweig and Buber, as was Jacob Agus, but at the same time he kept his own counsel, nurtured his own thoughts, and being a pragmatist, he brought his own philosophy to bear on the problems that agitate American Jewry. He was always the scholar and teacher; he initiated no movement, and did not seek to make disciples, and on some important issues, he at times courageously took a radical, unpopular stand. But his thoughts on practical questions always had a philosophic base; they were not spontaneous, emotional reactions; they were the results of deep soul searching, deep study, deep thought. To understand and appreciate his views on American Jewry, his ideology of American Judaism, it is essential to place these views against the background of his philosophic thought, where they have their roots. "All the decisions that we make out of the depths of our being," Agus wrote, "involve some reference to a philosophy of life, a grasp of the ultimate."[2]

Agus identified himself as belonging to the rationalist school of Jewish thought, at the head of which stands the great Maimonides. He believed that God revealed Himself not only in the Torah, but that He reveals Himself continuously "through the twin lights of conscience and intelligence"; that the written documents of revelation need to be interpreted by the mind and conscience; that the mind and conscience make the written word a living word, and that the primacy of this concept of the living word (not necessarily the written word) is the "central insight of Judaism."[3]

But Agus was no absolutist. We may have, he wrote, a glimpse of the absolute, but quickly added, "we can never possess the absolute."[4] And so it is that the rationalist must to a degree find accommodation for other approaches, including the romantic view of Judaism, such as that of Yehudah Halevi, the mystic approach of the Kabballah, and the legalistic approach. He liked to quote the saying of the sages that there are fifty gates of wisdom.[5] The rational mind is only one of the gates. Furthermore, any line of thought or argument must take into account the fact that it is not free from tensions, for the principle of polarity is ever operative. Thus ethnocentrism is countered by humanism; particularism is countered by universalism; emphasis on nationalism serves to trigger an added emphasis on religion; tradition at times must give way to creation.[6]

Agus took the principle of polarity from the philosopher Morris Raphael Cohen. This principle, Agus wrote,

> as formulated by Cohen, states that "opposites, such as immediacy and media-tion, unity and plurality, the fixed and the flux, substance and function, ideal and real, actual and possible" all enter into the pattern of our understanding. ... If only one polar concept is insisted upon as the one true principle, knowledge is reduced to absurdity.[7]

"Dynamic polarization," wrote Agus, "is the mark of a living faith."[8] Reference to the principle of polarization can be found in almost each of Agus's writings, for he firmly believed that "In nearly every human situation requiring an act of decision, a polarity of principles applies."[9] "Tension," he wrote, "is of the essence of living faith; there is hardly any phase of it that is not a reflection of a polarity."[10]

In his research, in his search for answers, Agus tread softly and humbly, ever hoping to hear "after the fire, a still small voice." For he believed that "at the base of human thought, lies the feeling of humble reverence.... There can be no cocksureness in matters of religion.... Often the restless agnostic comes nearer to genuine piety than the professional religionist. For piety is, at bottom, a seeking and a quest."[11]

Agus opposed theories of society that were derived from Darwin-ism and an emphasis on "biologism" and the struggle for existence; or from the Marxist theory of the class struggle; or from a Freudian psychologist. All such theories, he held, dehumanize, and degrade the human being, the human mind. Instead, Agus projected a "spirit-centered" conception of the human being and society. By this conception, he meant

> the unity of all values as they are unfolded in the course of man's quest for reality, a quest that alternates between the depths of subjectivity and the fur-thest reaches of objective reason.... The reality and validity of human values, esthetic, ethical, and religious, is the basic axiom, though the content and nature of any one value may be periodically re-examined. This axiom may also be called an assertion of faith, but it is that residual minimum of faith that our human nature invariably contains as it confronts the mystery of existence.[12]

Another central belief held by Agus was the centrality of ethics. Ethical values are the basis on which philosophy and religion must be based. In accord with the principle of polarity, it must be expected that other values will compete with ethics for recognition and even dominance, but, as we shall see, Agus seems to accord to ethical values the final word. Agus wrote that the "intuition" of the "objective validity" of ethical values "is the basis of my philosophy and religion." He wrote that "In moments of intense fervor, we feel that rightness and wrongness are eternally fixed in the scheme of things; that it is not our own personal dictates and impulses that are the source of ethical feeling; that the things we call 'good' and ' bad' are ... designated by the Eternal One, Who stands outside of us and yet dwells with us."[13]

Lastly, it remains to be mentioned that Agus was a staunch pluralist, especially as concerns religion. "Once we admit," he wrote, "that many ways lead to God, we no longer feel called upon to prove that only our faith, whatever it be, is true."[14] He did not feel that he needed to argue on behalf of a pluralistic position, for by now, he was persuaded, "the pluralistic articulation of the religious impulse is taken for granted."[15] Agus maintained that there must be openness to experiences, intuitions, thoughts, and approaches, from whatever source they may come. Even within one's own historical tradition there are a variety of views from which one may learn and benefit, and no one tradition has a monopoly on all the fifty gates of wisdom.[16]

These, I think, are the basic organizing principles or thoughts that Agus arrived at from his study of both Jewish and non-Jewish sources. As a student of William Ernest Hocking at Harvard, Agus was an avid student of comparative religion. "And what should they know of England who only England know?" Kipling asked. And Agus applied this thought to religion. We become fully aware of the meaning of our heritage, he wrote, "only as we learn to understand with sympathy the religion of our neighbor."[17]

This radical openness of mind and spirit Agus manifested in all his writings as he applied it to all problems and challenges. Typical of this approach and commitment is the way he considered the idea of chosenness, the belief in the principle of Israel as the Chosen People. This was a subject on which he wrote extensively, it crops up in almost each of his works. In Agus's mind, the concept of chosenness was inextricably tied to the idea of covenant, that the people of Israel were the Chosen People with whom God made a special covenant. Both ideas, Agus maintained, unfortunately lend themselves to the perversion of ethnocentrism. Agus tried to salvage these conceptions from the distortions to which they were exposed over the centuries.

Agus noted that the problem of a chosen people is not peculiar to Judaism, for every religious tradition and the impetus of nationalism tend toward the assertion of chosenness, a belief in its supreme value. Every religion and every nation in some way claims to be "a light unto all the nations."[18] In the Jewish tradition, however, the concept has manifested a polar tension between ethnocentrism and recognition of the wrongness or evil of exclusive claims to virtue or holiness. As between "the lofty heights of universalistic idealism" and "the dark depths of collective 'sacred egoism,'" Agus never hesitated to choose the former.[19]

In every possible context, Agus chose to remind his readers and students that the ancient rabbis maintained that God had made a covenant with the sons of Noah, to whom He had revealed seven laws of morality, known as the Noahchide Laws or the Seven Laws of Noah,[20] that constituted a universal revelation of morality and religion, a body of natural law and the essence of a natural religion. They also maintained that true prophets had risen among non-Jews, so that it is possible that there is more than one body of revealed laws. There were prophets in Israel who believed that God could conclude Torah-like covenants with other peoples, like Egypt and Assyria.[21] Agus quotes the following illuminating passage from Albo's *Safer Ha-Ikkarim*, the fifteenth-century classic:

> There is no doubt that the other nations attained human happiness through the Noachian law, since it is divine; though they could not reach the same degree of happiness as that attained by Israel through the Torah. The Rabbis say, "the pious men of the other nations have a share in the world to come." This shows that there may be two divine laws existing at the same time among different nations, and that each one leads those who live by it to attain human happiness.[22]

In a personal confession of faith published in 1981, Agus wrote that it was through the Jewish tradition that he grew up to feel the majesty and the message of God, a God who transcended nature and history. But the emphasis in Judaism on God's transcendence kept him from surrendering to the notion that God's will, in all its fullness, is reflected exclusively in his own tradition. Although he could live within the confines of his own tradition, he yet believed that "divine revelation in all its dimensions is universal and all-human."[23]

Agus was, of course, thoroughly familiar with the uncomfortable fact that there was another stream of teaching in Judaism that made an ethnocentric claim on the concept of chosenness and the concept of covenant, but he believed that there was ample warrant for the universalistic, open-ended line of interpretation, and so he concluded his "personal confession" by stating that he took the phrase "Chosen People" in Judaism to mean that the ideal Israel was to be and act as an *example* to others, individuals and nations, and not that Israel was an exception; that, in the words of Isaiah, Israel was meant to be "a covenanted people, a light to the nations."[24] The moral law is the essential message of the biblical prophets; linking that message with the Noahachide Laws makes ethical monotheism a religion open to non-Jews no less than to the Jewish people. Judaism therefore shares ethical monotheism with other monotheistic religions. The prophetic message and the Seven Laws of the Sons of Noah, by their very nature, give openness to Judaism. Agus quotes with approval the following statement from the Talmud, tractate Megillah: "Anyone who denies idolatry is called a Jew."[25] And Agus cites Maimonides as authority for the proposition that both Christianity and Islam are divine agencies that help prepare the way for the Messiah.[26]

Judaism, Agus contended, "is the central, all-pervasive and all-absorbing element of the civilization of the Jewish people."[27] By Judaism he meant the religion in its various, pluralistic expressions. But what does Agus make of Jewish nationhood? Agus wrote repeatedly on the subject of nationhood, which troubled him no end, but the conclusion he reached was not to deny nationhood entirely but to give it a minor role. "I believe," he wrote, "that the motive of nationalism [among Jews] is productive of good only when it is kept in the background, as subordinate to the universal ideals of ethics and religion."[28] The Jewish people have survived because of their religion; "the survival of the Jewish nationality was an effect rather than a cause."[29] Agus spoke of nationalism as a myth, "characterized by the assumption of a dark and mysterious 'national soul,' which is apprehended in intuition."[30] It is probably impossible to free ourselves completely from this myth, but it is most important, argued Agus, that we surmount the myth of nationality or ethnicity by emulating the prophetic example to deflate the myth as promptly as it arises.[31] For the prophet is the foe "of self-glorifying ethnicism, of self-sanctifying dogmatism, of human arrogance in all its subtle variations."[32]

III

The principles, concepts, and beliefs that we have thus far discussed, notably the concepts of covenant, chosenness, the centrality of religion, the subordinate role of nationality, the primacy of ethical values, pluralism—Agus brought to bear on the status and future of Jews in the United States. It is not possible to tell from his extensive writings which came first, his thoughts on religion and Judaism, his thoughts on nationalism, ethics, that he then applied to the American Jewish scene, or that he derived his general conceptions from what he thought about American Jewry. In all likelihood, all his thoughts were intertwined, for he was a student of rabbinics and of philosophy, a rabbi and a teacher-scholar, throughout his adult years. At the same time that he was a congregational rabbi, he was also a college professor; he wrote his treatises and books at the same time that he thought about his sermons.

As Agus looked upon the American Jewish scene, he saw that secularism and Zionism, and a Zionism that was secularist and a Zionism that was, in his words, "dressed up in dubious religious garb,"[33] are inherently nationalistic. But, he held, "As an independent motive, sheer nationalism—especially as 'normalized' since the establishment of the State of Israel, can only lead either in the direction of headlong assimilation or toward the status of a racist minority."[34] The military victories of Israel have given an emotional boost to Jewish pride, and may have worked to remove an inferiority obsession, but this may only stimulate the drive to assimilation. The important truth is, said Agus, "that the national impulse, as such, is not, capable of functioning in America as a goal of Jewish living."[35] Jewish nationalism, however, when subordinated to higher considerations "may continue to be a powerful creative force, serving the ends of Jewish religion, as it did in the past, by bringing to the aid of piety additional motivation, and by supplying foci of sentimental loyalty within the Jewish community."[36] But Agus repeatedly stressed the belief, to which he firmly adhered, that the nationalist ideal, if elevated to the status of a supreme goal or value, can only lead American Jews into a dead-end, "since it cannot offer a worthy *raison d'être* for American Jewish life."[37] When made into a supreme goal, Jewish nationalism would have the tragic end of relegating Jewry to the status of a self-segregating racist minority that would reject the goal of immigrant assimilation, although assimilation is "the natural end of other immigrant nationalists in America."[38]

The relegation of American Jewry into a nationality or an ethnic entity would mean to Christians that Jews persist in being a nation within a nation, a foreign element, an enclave "unabsorbed and alien." In such a case, it is reasonable to expect American gentiles to ask why do the Jews remain here, why do they not go to their national home-land, the State of Israel?[39]

It was Agus's firm belief that there was no future for a variety of ethnicisms in American life. "For the ineluctable fact is," he wrote, "that the *natural* tendency for all national groups is to dissolve and disappear within the American melting pot." Here and there one may still see colonies of European nationalities continuing in the "isolation of self-imposed ghettos," but they are the exception to "the mighty expanse of America's mainstream life. The bland assumption that Jewry is a national entity does not protect American Israel against the absorptive effects of the melting pot."[40]

The stereotype of the Jew as an unassimilable element can only be strengthened in the mind of the non-Jew if the latter would take seri-ously the classic Zionist claim that the Jewish homeland is intended to gather in all the Jews of the Diaspora, but this can be avoided only

> if it is made sun-clear that the intention in establishing the homeland was not at all the evacuation of American Jewry... but the founding of a haven of refuge for the persecuted Jews in other lands, and the creation of a cultural-religious center for World Jewry. In that case the emergence of a new type of "produc-tive" and fighting Jew will help to banish the time-worn Jewish stereotype from the minds of Christians, and ... aid the American Jew to accept his Jewish origin with pride and his religious heritage with ease and naturalness, as all other Americans accept their origin and religions. To this end the theses of Herzlian Zionism must be repudiated insofar as American Jewry is concerned....We are led, irresistibly, then, to emphasize the religious purpose of Jewish group survival in this country.[41]

Agus quoted with approval the statement by Robert Gordis that "A secularist who is a Zionist must, if he is logically consistent, become a *Sholel Hagolah*, a negation of a Jewish future in the Diaspora."[42] Accordingly, in American Jewish life the movement must be "from ethnicism to Judaism". Ethnic feelings and loyalties must be directed into religious channels,[43] and the synagogue must become the center of Jewish life. But if this is to happen, the Jewish religion must not be viewed as a static body of dogmas, "but the upward surge of the human personality in all its fullness, and the Synagogue-center" must "embrace under its wings every cultural and uplifting interest of the Jewish community," and include in its program social, recreational, and all kinds of cultural activities. Its message should be, "nothing that is Jewish or human is alien to me."[44]

Agus, of course, recognized the fact that large numbers of Jews are not affiliated with synagogues or temples. Many of them are spiritually sensitive persons "whose entire being is profoundly stirred by Jewish associations and problems." How, he asked rhetorically, can they be termed "marginal" without a perversion of Jewish values? In addition, there are, he recognized, "masses of indifferent materialists," who are, in one way or another, included in the Jewish organizational complex, but who are unmoved by any kind of appeal to spiritual values. What does one do about them? Agus answered by saying,

> The moral task before us, then, is to transmute deep ethnic consciousness into reawakened dedication to the ideals and values of the Jewish spirit. We must chart a path from the sense of being part of an embattled camp to the sense of being a partner of the Lord in the creation of a world patterned after His Word.[45]

As appears, Agus saw a distinction between Jews who are spiritually sensitive and Jews who are both spiritually sensitive and religious. If the synagogue would stress the ethical and spiritual ideals and values of Judaism, a bridge may be established between the non-religious spiritually sensitive Jews and the religious community.

> By cleaving to the spiritual interpretation of Jewish experience we provide a means for the non-religious among us to progress in the realm of the spirit through their Jewish identification. To be sure, we have not shown how the gulf in many men's minds between adherence to spiritual values and the convictions of religion may be bridged. There is in fact a plus of conviction in religious faith, with regard to the roots in eternity of spiritual values, which cannot be obtained by the cultivation of a humanist attitude alone. Spiritually minded people will still find congregational life the best means of continuing their own spiritual progress, through self-identification with Jewish experience in the religious interpretation, and by promoting its values in the religious interpretation, and by promoting its values in the social grouping of which they are a part.[46]

As Agus surveyed the Jewish scene in the United States and in Israel, the two main centers of Jews after the Holocaust, he saw that "In Israel the Jews are becoming a secular nationality, with the ancient faith as a subordinate reality, while in America, the Jews are becoming a religious denomination, with an ethnic underside."[47] This may mean that the Jewish people may be falling apart into separate peoples. The tragic separation can be avoided by many factors but chiefly if the Jewish tradition will continue as a living appeal to the members of the Jewish family:

> So long as that tradition is cultivated and made part of the lives of successive generations, the family will be a living reality. Every son and daughter need only be concerned with his own relation to the spiritual treasure of the family--does he [or she] cherish it and live by its light? The unity of a widely scattered family is the product of the loyalty of its members to their common tradition.[48]

Since the Jewish tradition is the Jewish religion, with only an underside of ethnicity, it is, in the final analysis, only a spiritual-ethical-universalistic Judaism that can keep the Jewish people together as a single family, both in Israel and the Diaspora.

Agus naturally viewed the situation as a worrisome one. Yet he moved from pessimism to optimism, and from optimism to pessimism. He was fully aware of the secularization and assimilation forces in America, and of the deep gulf between the religious community in Israel and the majority of its population. Yet he saw merit in the conception of the late Solomon Rawidowitz that Israel and America may constitute two centers of Judaism. With this thought in mind, Agus wrote,

> It is as impossible for the Jews of Israel to think of themselves completely in secular terms, ignoring the burden of the all-Jewish tragedy and the import of ancestral faith, as it is for American Jewry to proclaim itself to be just another religious denomination. Inescapably, the past is reclaimed by every living generation, though in varying interpretations.

The conclusion he drew is that it is the burden of the Jewish intellectuals in both Israel and America to pattern the diverse elements of the Jewish tradition in such a way that the result will be a synthesis "that is meaningful and elevating for the people of a particular time and place."[49]

For American Jews, Agus saw in Christianity a wholesome challenge, a call to Jews to break down "the self-exalting impetus of ethnicism and to caution against the externalization of religion and its hardening into a series of lifeless rituals." And for American Christians Agus saw Judaism challenging them to make the world "more prophetic, more communal minded, more rational and ethical, more concerned with the 'works' of love."[50]

American Jews need have no fear of contact with the Christian community. Judaism, Agus believed, attained its highest intellectual levels when it was in contact with foreign civilizations. "In history, as in nature, productivity springs from the intermingling of cultures and influences. Isolationism in thought is sterile, as it is inane and futile in politics."[51]

But what of anti-Semitism? Agus believed that "the battle of anti-defamation is waning into insignificance, primarily for lack of anti-Semites to combat." Of course, one cannot be absolutely certain that anti-Semitism will never again be aroused, but there are certain objective factors working against this ugly possibility; first, the anti-Semitic ideology fostered by Nazism has been thoroughly discredited; second, the creation of the State of Israel robs that ideology of the stereotype of the "wandering Jew"—the Jew is now normalized, no longer the mysterious alien. And so, once again Agus draws the conclusion, "In relative freedom from the virulent sting of anti-Semitism, we may expect the pattern of Jewish loyalties to shift ever more decisively from the pole of ethnicism to the one of a personal faith."[52]

American Jews and Christians cannot be indifferent to one another; they must be in a dialogue relationship. Jews and Christians can come together as religious humanists, and discover how the respective traditions can be harmonized "with that universal, growing truth in which all of us share."[53] The dialogue will not end in a syncretism but in a new openness.[54] For we must remember the words of Micah: "For all the peoples walk every one in the name of his god, and we will walk in the name of the Lord our God for ever and ever."[55] Such a relationship will be an expression and reaffirmation of American religious pluralism.[56]

Agus disparaged the idea of a secular Jewish culture for American Jews. Immigrant Jews needed a Jewish culture before they became acculturated to the American civilization. That was a temporary phenomenon, satisfying a nostalgic longing for the past: "Insofar as secular 'Jewish culture' attempts to supply the same values as American culture, it is superfluous. ... Hence, to saddle a secular 'Jewish culture' upon the American Jew is just as gratuitous as to lumber him with an additional national allegiance."[57] Agus was quite emphatic on this point: "The only healthy function of the Jewish heritage in the American Jew is to supply the element of religion. American life is culturally monolithic but religiously pluralistic." Judaism as a religion changes the image of the Jew from being simply a "non-Aryan" to a "son [or daughter] of the living God."

The image of the Jew thus perceived can find expression in scholarship, literature, music, and art, which can constitute a distinctive reli-

gious culture "as distinguished from the phony secular 'Jewish culture.'" The latter is both superfluous and inferior. "And it is preposter-
ous to speak of the works of every writer, painter and musician who
happens to have been born a Jew, but is devoid of Judaism, as constituting 'Jewish culture.' "[58]

But it would be a grave mistake to conclude from the above pas-
sages that Agus believed that the Jews in America constituted merely
just another religious minority. The Jews, he contended, are a special
kind of minority, not just a religious minority, nor just an ethnic
minority. "Ours is more than a creed, more than a so-called 'way of
life,' more than even the ethnic-cultural ties of a people. *We are the
living bearers of a tradition that both supplements and corrects the
one-sidedness of the Christian tradition.*"[59] Jews in America can be a
"creative minority." Repudiating only those who negate the value of
the American Diaspora and those who are "Zion-centered," American
Jews can place their emphasis on "autonomy, on creativeness," and
cherish and foster "whatever cultural and spiritual values are generated by every individual interpretation, every aspiration, within
the community." While conscious of its own distinguishing attributes, this creative minority will sense "its underlying and essential unity with the general population," and it will not feel
itself isolated, for its history and tradition "constitute a vital part
of the realm of ideas and experience upon which American civilization is based. Thus we are part of Christian culture, though apart from
it," for the "Judeo-Christian tradition" forms "the spiritual substratum of
Western civilization."[60]

Furthermore, as a creative minority, the Jewish community can
expand the cultural horizons of all Americans by developing the truths
that are implicit in its peculiar status, and thus unfold fresh insights
for the guidance of all Americans. Finally, as a creative minority the
Jewish community is value-centered and oriented toward the future,
toward "the sunlight of spiritual growth."[61] All this can be accomplished "through the impetus of our specific religious-cultural tradition in continuous interaction with the Christian tradition."[62]

This line of argument, by its inherent forceful logic, led Agus to
the conclusion that the Jews in America are on the way to become
"*Jewish Americans.*" What was adjectival becomes substantive, and
what was substantive becomes adjectival. *American Jews* will become *Jewish Americans*:

> If to be at home is not only to be in possession of' "rights" but also to be part
> of the people to whose service the political machinery of the state is dedicated,
> then the Jew can be here utterly at home, thinking of himself as an American of
> the Jewish faith, as "normal" in the civil sense of the term as any other citizen
> of the great country.

Agus was, of course, fully aware that not every Jew would embrace the change from the genus "Jew living in America" to that of "Jewish American." "The Jewishly ignorant and the embittered, the eager opportunists and the dust-dry rationalists, the rootless intellectuals and the witless hangers-on will be likely to desert our ranks in a steady procession." On the other hand, however, Jews will find ways to express themselves in positive acts of identification, for being a Jew will no longer mean falling into a category automatically with or without one's will. Because the American pattern is that of a nation that unifies multiple faiths—*e pluribus Unum*—"Jewish loyalty will derive accessions of strength from both the pervasive atmosphere of American culture and the momentum of the Jewish tradition."

> Standing at the threshold of the fourth century of Jewish life in America, we
> can foresee the progressive "normalization" of Jewish feeling: hence, the shrink-
> ing of the ethnic strands of loyalty, the forging of ever stronger bonds of
> fraternity with the American people, and the steady growth of the ideal and
> religious components of Judaism.[63]

IV

In September 1789, during the French Revolution, deputies in the Constituent Assembly were alarmed by the report from Alsace that peasants had attacked Jews. Count Stanislas de Clermont-Tonnerre demanded that the Assembly act to extend protection to the Jews, and several months later, when the debate about the Jewish question was resumed, he stated that the rights of the Jews had been implicitly recognized by the Declaration of the Rights of Man, which states that no person shall be persecuted for his or her religion. In the course of his speech, Clermont-Tonnerre declared: "Jews should be denied everything as a nation, but granted everything as individuals."[64] Seventeen years later, when Napoleon Bonaparte considered the situation of the 40,000 Jews who lived in France, he saw that they constituted a "nation within a nation," and he instituted measures that would change their condition, that would confer civil rights on them as individuals, but abolish their "national" character.[65]

Despite these measures and other developments, we know from the recent tragic history that Jews in France and in Germany were hated and looked upon as an element that could never be assimilated. This was due to the fact, noted by Agus, that Germans and Frenchmen considered themselves as constituting nations by a blood relationship; that they were, in some sense, natural "races," nations by birth:

> The romantic-reactionary circles in Europe [in the time of the French Revolution and in the Napoleonic period] tended generally to demand the ultimate disappearance of the Jewish group as the condition for emancipation. Doubtless, too, they echoed in this the unexpressed feelings of the masses that, for the most part, were able to think of brotherhood only in biological terms as blood-kinship.[66]

This emphasis on the biological basis of nationalism made it impossible for Jews to become an integral part of any European nation-state.[67]

The situation in America, Agus contended, is quite different. Although the possibility of an intensified anti-Semitism cannot be altogether ruled out, there are good reasons to believe that what happened in Europe will not happen here:

> The indubitable fact, enshrined in the memory of the American nation, of its having arisen out of a mixture of races and nationalities, interposes a supreme obstacle to the emergence here of a romantic blood-based brand of nationalism, with its corollary of racist anti-Semitism. America is the one great state where the emergence of the nation did not precede the formation of the state. The American nation came into being, in fact, as a massive protest against the voice of blood by the voice of reason and morality.[68]

This is a persuasive line of argument. Certainly America is different from the European nations, where today almost throughout the continent nationalities make unsettling demands of self-determination, demands for nationalisms based on birth and blood. But in the United States today we also hear shrieking voices that demand racial and ethnic self-determination, a search for "roots"; a clamor for "multiculturalism" that is mostly a euphemism for racialism and ethnicism; a demand for cultural pluralism but without the orchestration of the pluralism into a national unity, for a *pluribus* but not for e *pluribus Unum*.[69]

The American ideal was an *orchestrated* pluralism of cultures and not a segregation of ethnic, national, or religious groupings. We see the present-day demands and their tendency, and the picture is far from reassuring, For in many instances we see public and private educational systems and institutions capitulating to the strident voices and compulsive demands.[70] The character of American demography is undergoing radical changes, and what these changes will do to the American ethos is impossible to say. It may well be, this much one may hazard to say, that in the resulting maelstrom, the only safety net for American Jewry may be the claim of being a religious minority.

And the demography of American Jewry is also undergoing radical, and deeply disturbing, changes. The National Jewish Population Survey, sponsored by the Council of Jewish Federations, based on the screening of over 125,000 randomly selected households across the United States, with a follow-up survey of those who met the screening criteria, showed a core of 5.5 million Jews defined by birth or religion. An additional 625,000 persons identified themselves as Jews by ethnic background or preference while identifying themselves as practicing a religion other than Judaism. In addition, some 700,000 children were identified as Jews by parentage or ethnic background but who were practicing a religion other than Judaism. There is a category comprising some 1.4 million born non-Jews who were part of households with at least one Jewish member.[71]

Another survey of Jewish demography released in 1991 and commissioned by the Graduate School of the City University of New York, that polled 113,000 households throughout the continental United States, found that 12 percent identified themselves as Christian, and another 22 percent said that they had no religion or were identified as belonging to a non-Christian faith. This means that one-third of American Jews are no longer Jews by religion. These findings show that American Jews are rapidly assimilating by conversion or by intermarriage or by shedding all religious belief.

Agus was aware of the problem and the challenge that it presents. His response was rational rather than emotional. What he wrote on this deeply disturbing subject needs to be quoted at length:

> Only liberal Jews can bring to an intermarried couple a message of self-acceptance based on genuine feelings of mutual reverence. From the liberal standpoint, the core of faith is the same in all forms of enlightened religion. Hence, devotees of different religions need not confront each other with the implacable

choice of *either* one religion or the other. They can view their own faith and that of their marriage partner in the spirit of "mine and thine."

To the Jewish member of the marriage, liberal Judaism can bring an interpretation that represents the Jew as an integral member of Western society and
Judaism as a creative element in Western civilization. The Jew could learn to
accept his heritage as one of the most important sources of enlightened religion
and modern culture. The non-Jewish partner could simultaneously learn to
accept the Jewish memories and loyalties of the Jewish partner as positive aids
to the creation of an atmosphere of religious dedication in their in their home.
Similarly, the Jewish partner could learn to recognize the essence of his liberal
faith in the religious heritage of his non-Jewish partner. The children could
learn to acquire a positive attitude to both religious traditions of their parents.
When they reach adulthood, they will choose to identify themselves with one
or the other religious community. Whatever their choice, they will possess a
warm appreciation of the Jewish faith. On their pilgrimage through life, they
will be sustained by a sense of wholehearted identification with *both* religious
traditions of their parents. Perhaps, too, they will recognize themselves-to be
peculiarly suited for the role of overcoming the multiple barriers of hate and
prejudice that still plague our society. At the present time [1971], this vast
marginal group of possibly half a million people is totally neglected by the
Jewish community. Here is a task of vast proportions for liberal Judaism to
undertake.[72]

One may reasonably question that this is a realistic view of the situation—either thirty years ago or at present. Agus described an ideal intermarried couple maintaining an ideal home where there is a maximum of love, understanding, and tender consideration. There probably are some families that approximate perfection, but such are a small minority. The ideal picture, however, is a tribute to Jacob Agus's equally maintained liberal spirit and reasoned consideration, and the fact that he invariably had the courage to say what he thought without resort to circumlocutions, indirections, or obliquities. It may be said of him that he was a Jewish American, for he felt himself to be fully and comfortably at home in America, where he could be and was fully and happily a Jew. And it may be said of him that he was, indeed, an American Jew, for the Jew defined the substance of the man, while his Americanism was only adjectival; that although he was an assimilated American, he was in no sense an assimilated Jew.

The principle of polarity that played so large a role in his thinking can be readily applied to Agus himself, for he was a hyphenated American and a hyphenated Jew, and so was never free of tension. He was both attached and detached, both rooted and transient, both a priest and a prophet, a man at home and a man who was a stranger;

someone who saw the possible as he looked at the actual, and saw always the ineluctable tension between the actual and the possible.[73] "Whatever drove or lured or guided him—a vision answering a faith unshaken."[74]

Notes

1. *Agus, Modern Philosophies of Judaism* (1941), 388, hereinafter referred to as *Modern Philosophies*. Cf. *Encyc. Judaica* 12:1014.
2. Agus, *Dialogue and Tradition* (1981), IX, hereinafter referred to as *Dialogue.*
3. Agus, *The Evolution of Jewish Thought* (195S), 410-411, hereinafter referred to as *Evolution.*
4. *Dialogue*, IX, 30-31, 65, 357.
5. *The Jewish Quest* (1983), 12; Rosh Hashonah 21b.
6   Agus, *Meaning of Jewish History*, 2 vols. (1963), II, 458, 462, 473, 477 hereinafter referred to as *Meaning.*
7. Agus, *Guideposts in Modern Judaism* (1954), hereinafter referred to as *Guideposts*, 236-237.
8. *Meaning*, 477.
9. *Dialogue*, IX.
10. Ibid, 432.
11. *Guideposts*, 347
12. *Dialogue*, 376.
13. *Guideposts*, 340-341.
14. *Dialogue!* 36.
15. *Quest*, 12.
16. *Dialogue*, 92.
17. Ibid., 508
18. *Evolution*, 420.
19. Ibid., 400.
20. *Dialogue*, 540. Av. Zora 64b; Sanhedrin 56a; Maimonides, Melhakim 8:10.
21. Isaiah 19:24. Cf. Micah, ch. 4.
22. *Dialogue* 472. The passage from Albo is from the translation by Isaac Husik, vol. I, ch. 25, 1978. See also Agus, "The Covenant Concept," *Journal of Ecumenical Studies* (Spring 1981), 18:226.
23. Agus, "Covenant Concept," note 22 supra, at 229.
24. Ibid., 230. Cf. Konvitz, "Many Are Called and Many Are Chosen," *Judaism* 4 (Winter 1955) 58.
25. *Quest*, 116, Megillah 138.
26. *Quest*, 56, Hilchot Melakim, ch. 11, uncensored version. See also p. 193, note 9.See Maimonides Reader, I. Twersky, ed. 1972, 226-227.
27. *Modern Philosophies*, 350.
28. Ibid, 357.
29. *Guideposts*, 326-327.
30. *Dialogue*, 373.
31. Ibid. 378.
32. Ibid. 381.
33. *Guideposts*, 178.34. Ibid.35.

35. Ibid.
36. Ibid.
37. Ibid.,179.
38. Ibid.
39. Ibid., 186.
40. Ibid., 145.
41. Ibid., 186-187.
42. Ibid., 196
43. Ibid., 414.
44. Ibid., 17.
45. Ibid., 197-198.
46. Ibid., 201.
47. *Meaning*, II, 483.
48. Ibid., 484.
49. Ibid., 452.
50. *Evolution*, 415.
51. *Guideposts*, 303-304.
52. *Dialogue*, 14.
53. Ibid., 27.
54. *Quest*, 121.
55. *Dialogue*, 28. Micah 4:5.
56. *Dialogue*, 28.
57. *Guideposts*, 159-160.
58. Ibid., 162.
59. Ibid., 208-209, italics in original.
60. Ibid., 213-215.
61. Ibid., 215.
62. Ibid.
63. *Dialogue*, 578-580, 587, 588.
64. *Encyc. Judaica* 5:605-606. *Dialogue*, 22, 57 95. *Guideposts*, 164.
65. *Encyc. Judaica* 7:23. *Dialogue* 582.
66. *Guideposts*, 164.
67. Ibid., 166.
68. Ibid., 168.
69. See Konvitz, editor, *Legacy of H. M. Kallen* (1987).
70. See Dinesh D'Souza, "The New Segregation," *American Scholar*, Winter 1991, 17; also D'Souza, *Illiberal Education* (1991). See also Edward Alexander, "Multiculturalism: The Jewish Question," *Forward*, Aug. 16, 1991.
71. *Amer. Jewish Yearbook* 1991, 206.
72. *Dialogue*, 566.
73. Cf. Konvitz, "Of Exile and Double Consciousness," *Encounter* (October 1980), 82-83.
74. Edwin Arlington Robinson, "The Man against the Sky."

Index